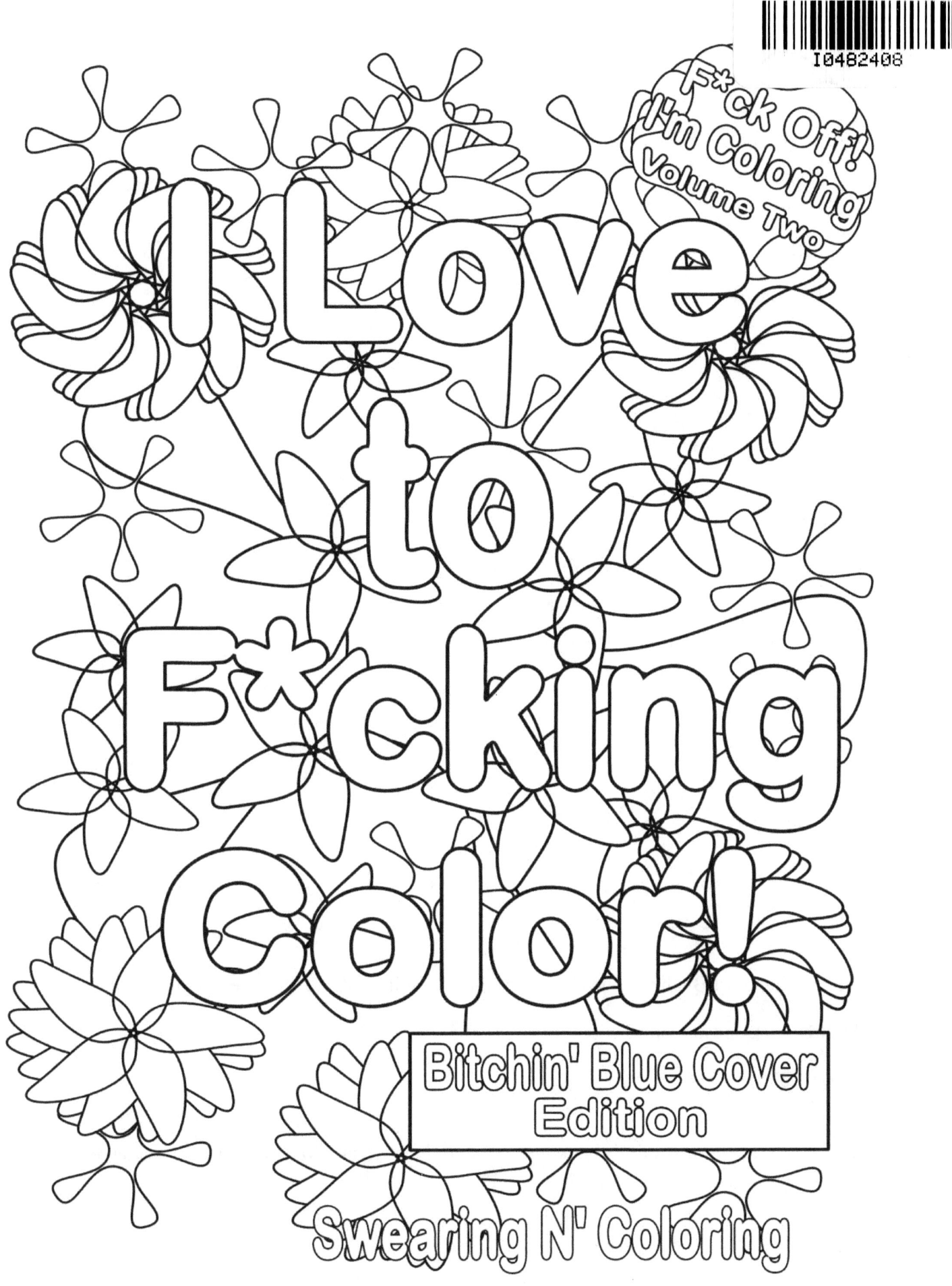

I Love to F*cking Color!

F*ck Off! I'm Coloring Volume Two

Bitchin' Blue Cover Edition

Swearing N' Coloring

I Love to F*cking Color! Bitchin' Blue Cover Edition: A Delightfully Dirty Swear Word Adult Coloring Book
Copyright 2016 by Don Cummings

ISBN-13: 978-1533557179
ISBN-10: 1533557179

20 Unique Swear Word Designs!

All Illustrations Are Printed Twice! Double The Fun!

Every Design Is On A Separate Piece Of Paper! No Bleed Through!

Hours And Hours Of Relaxation! Excellent Stress Relief!

Use Your Own Coloring Tools! Crayons, Colored Pencils, Or Markers!

Start Coloring Right Away!

Fuck Yeah!!!

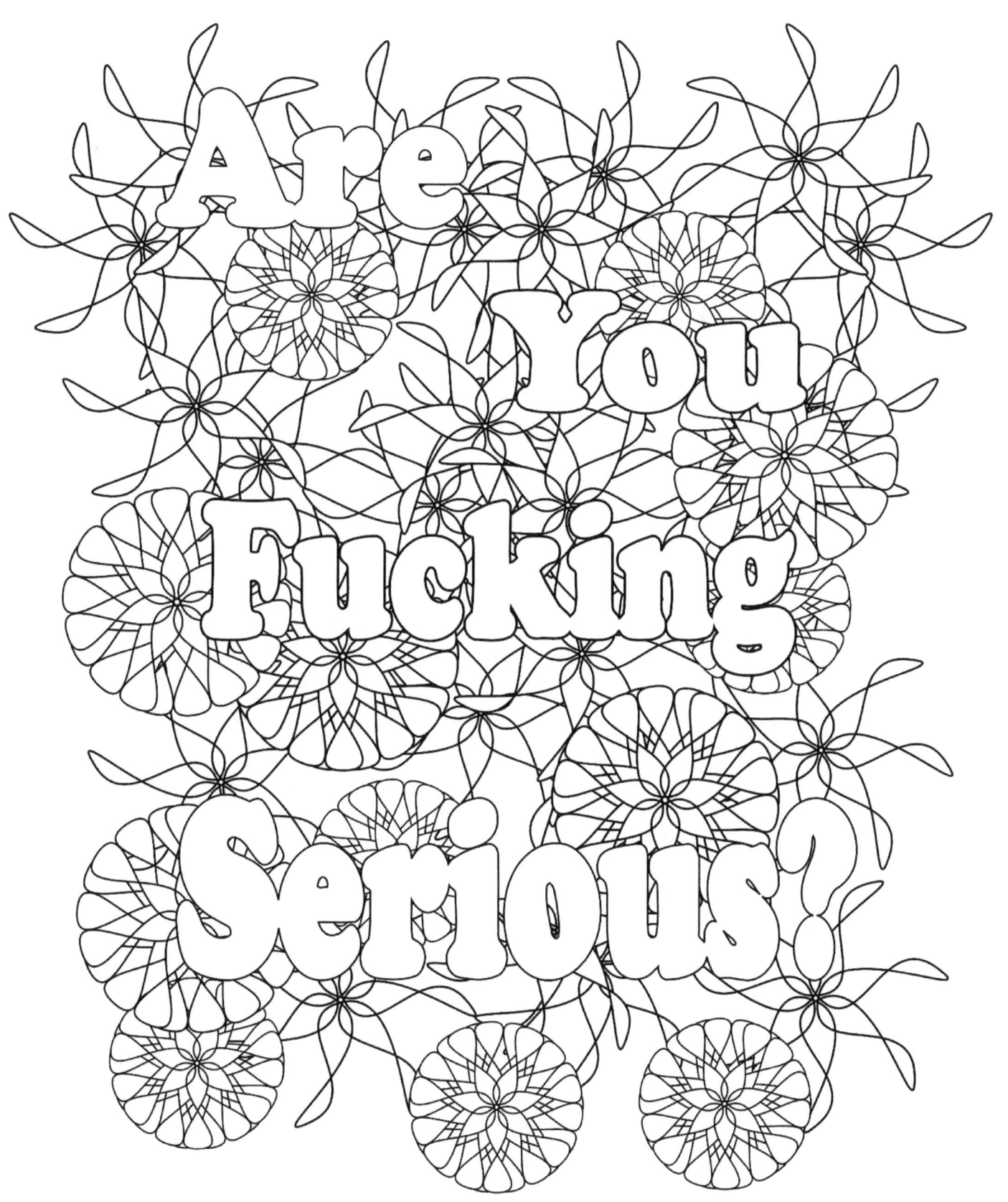

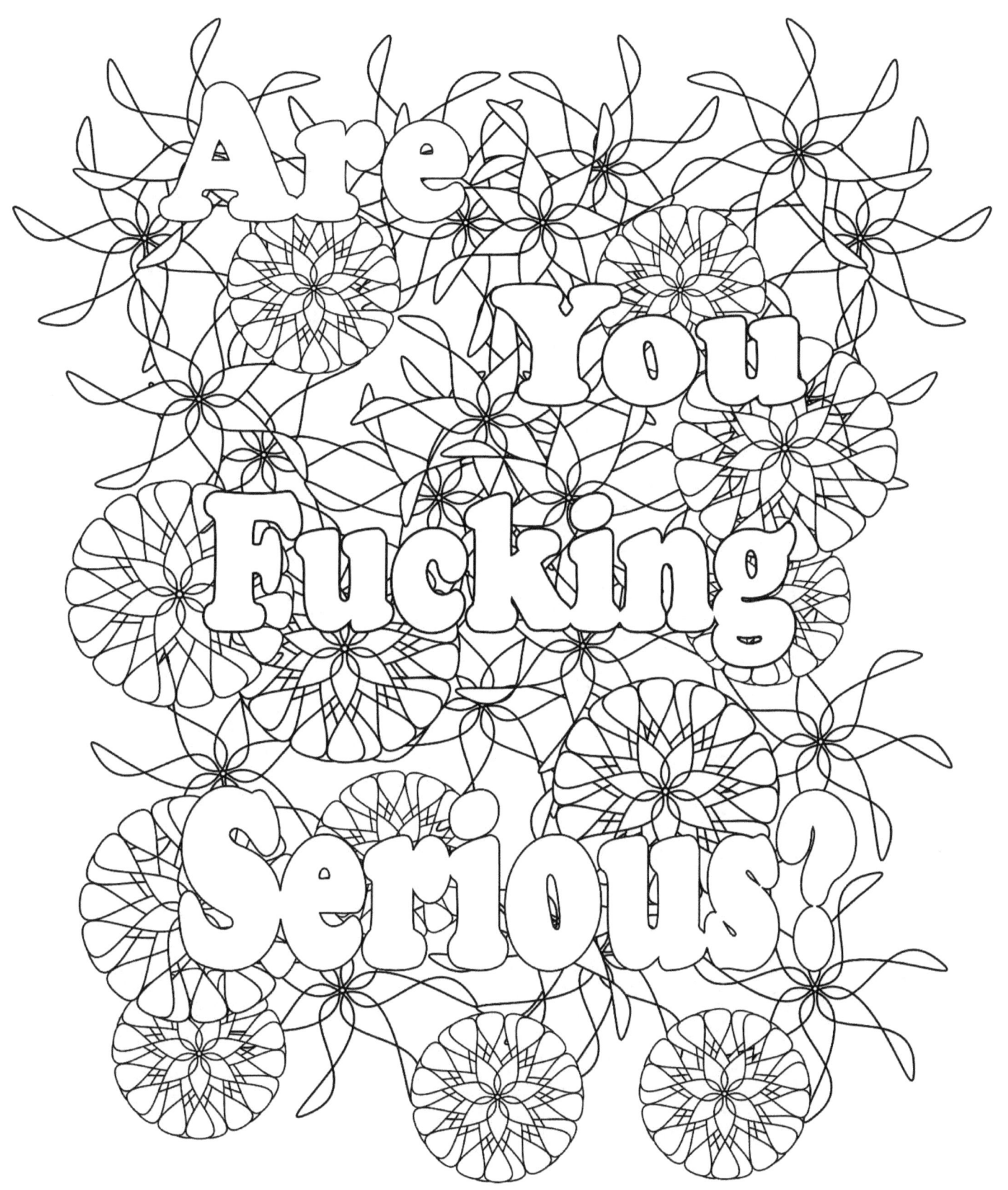

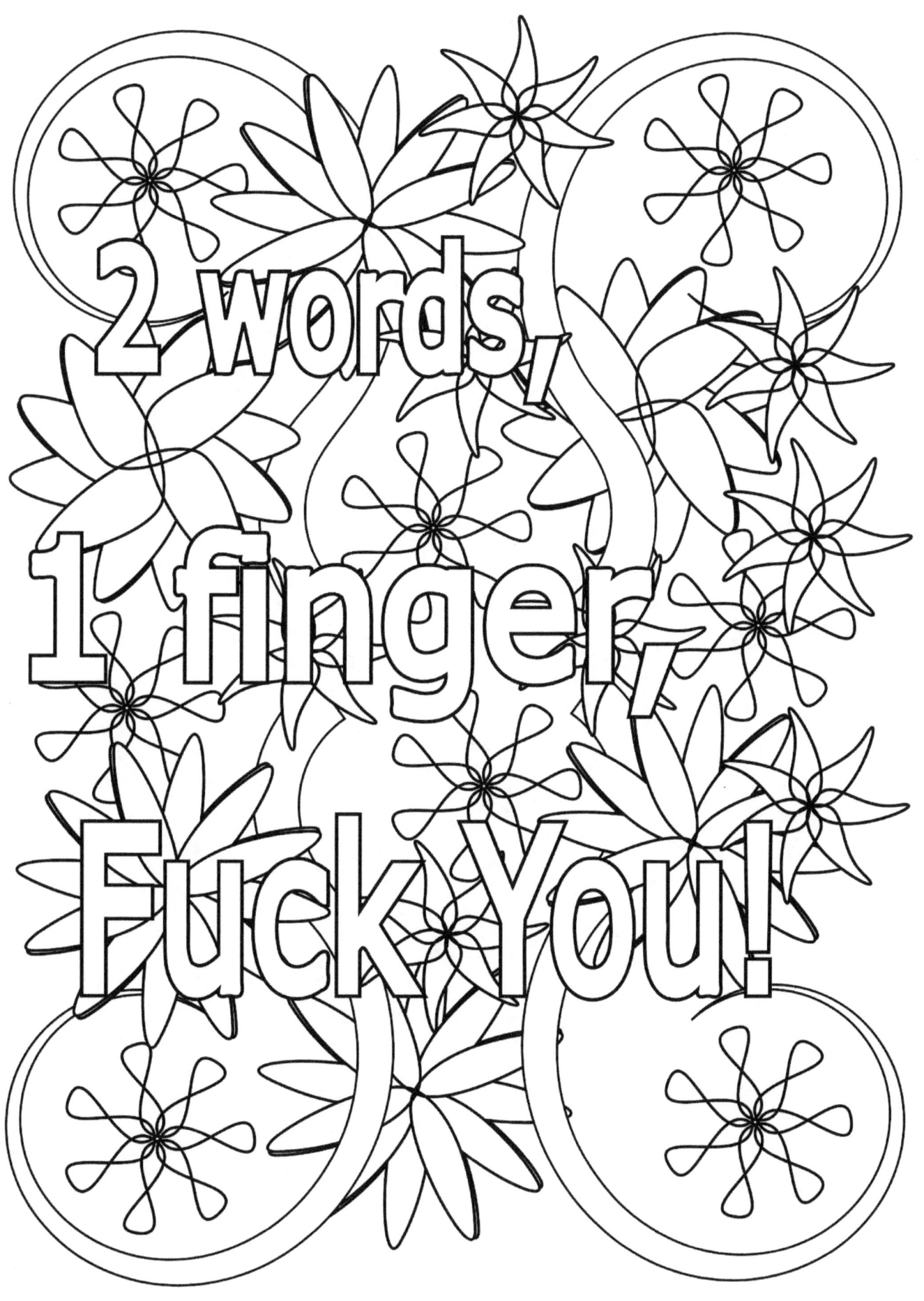

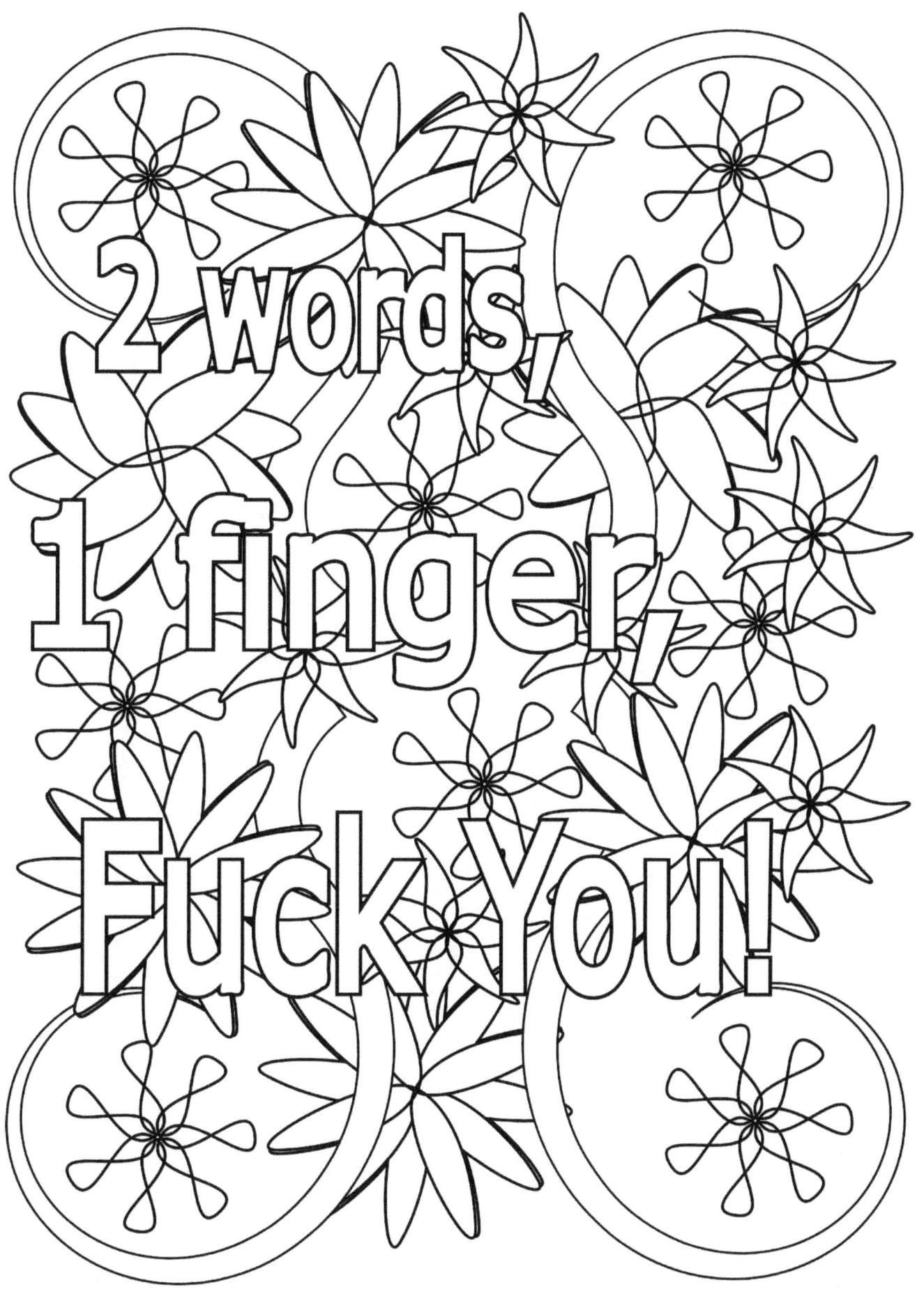

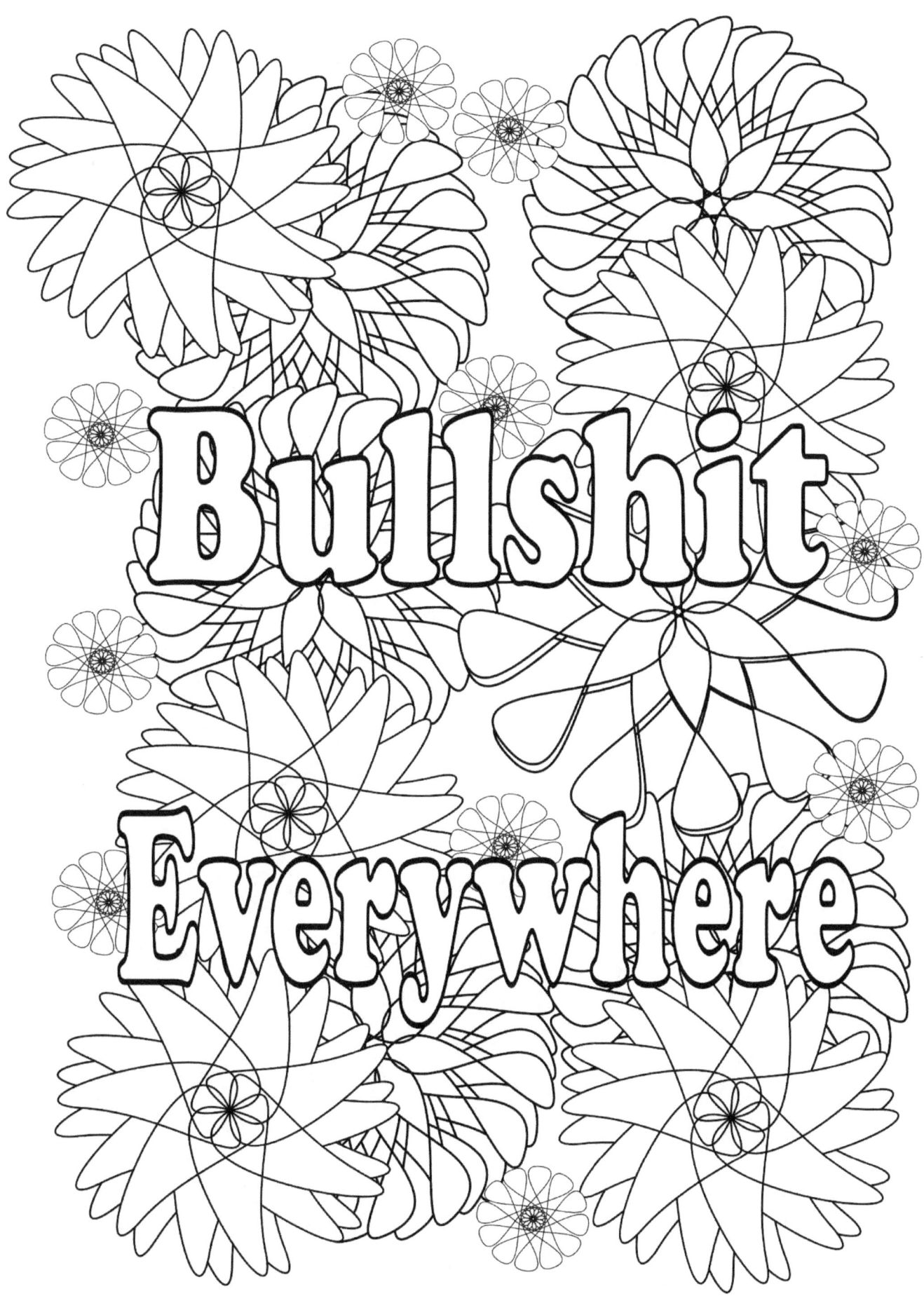

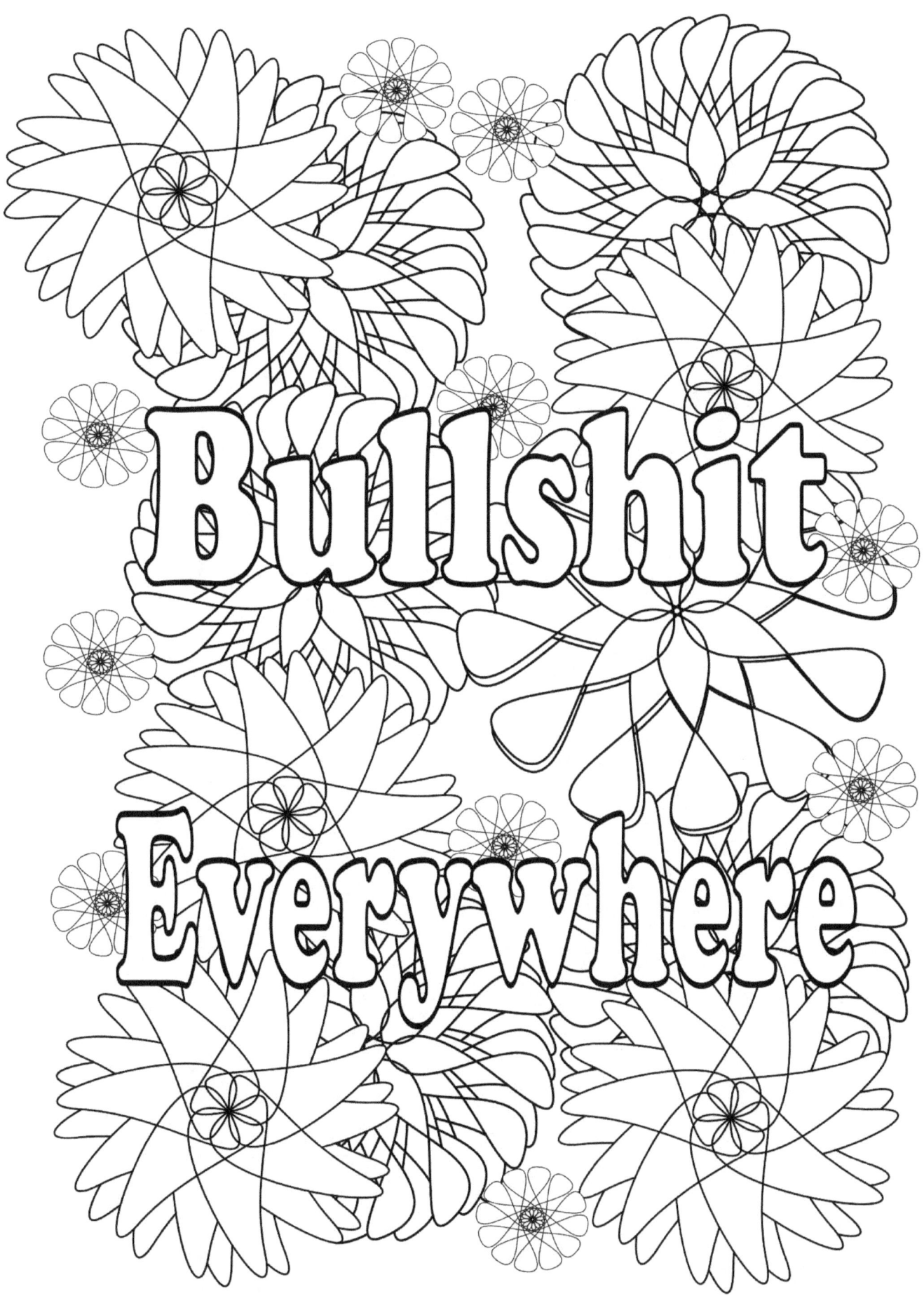

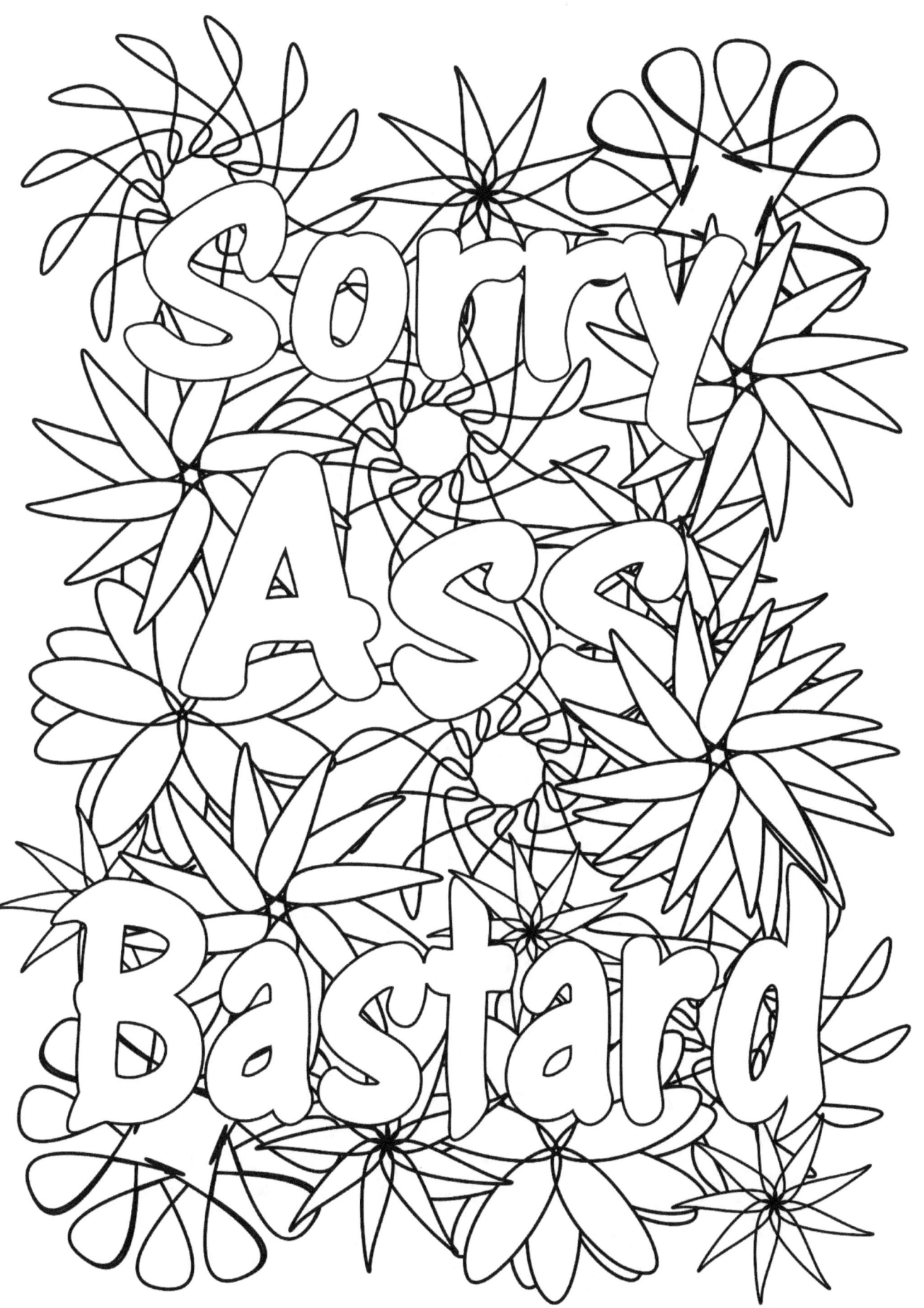

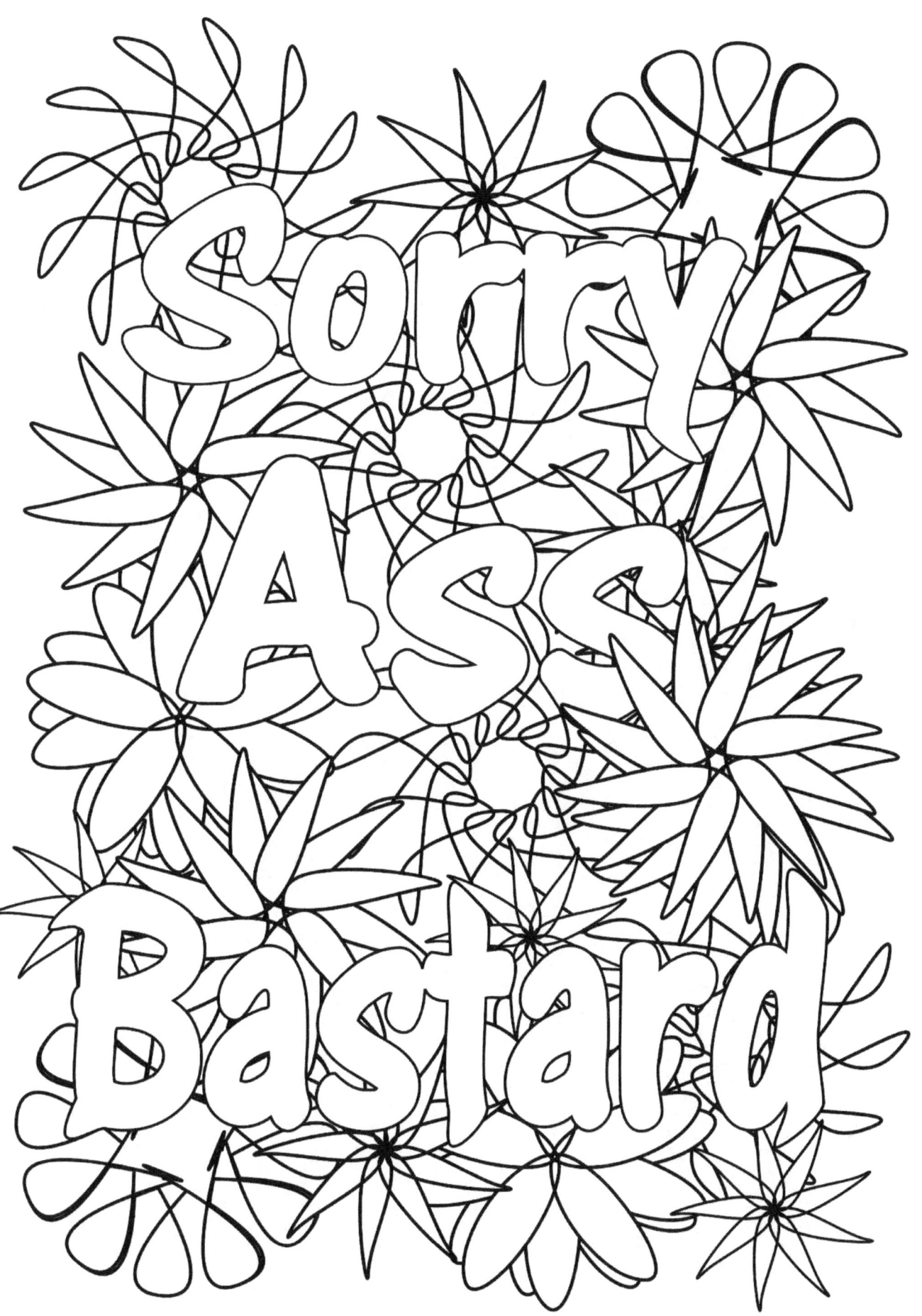

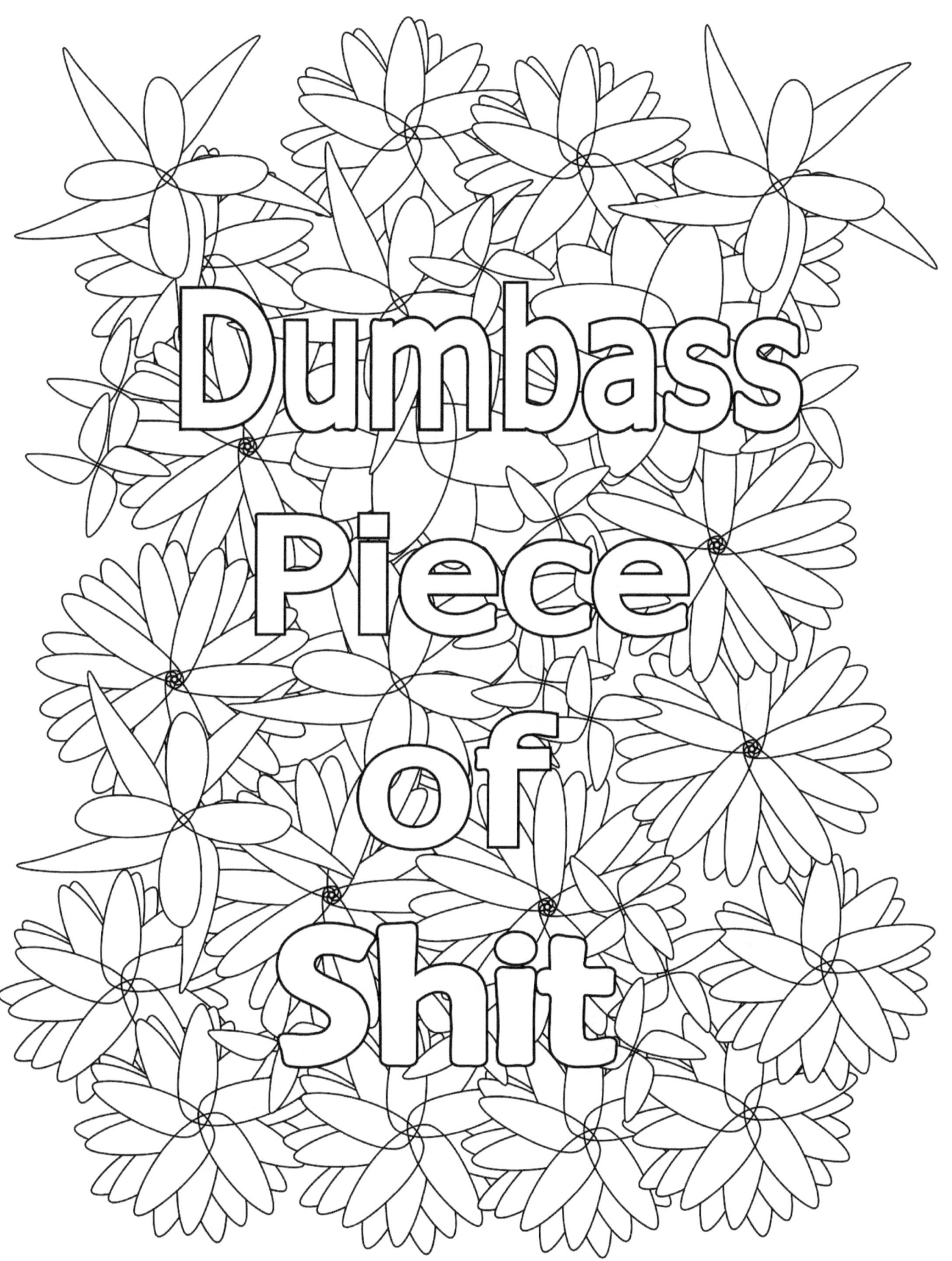

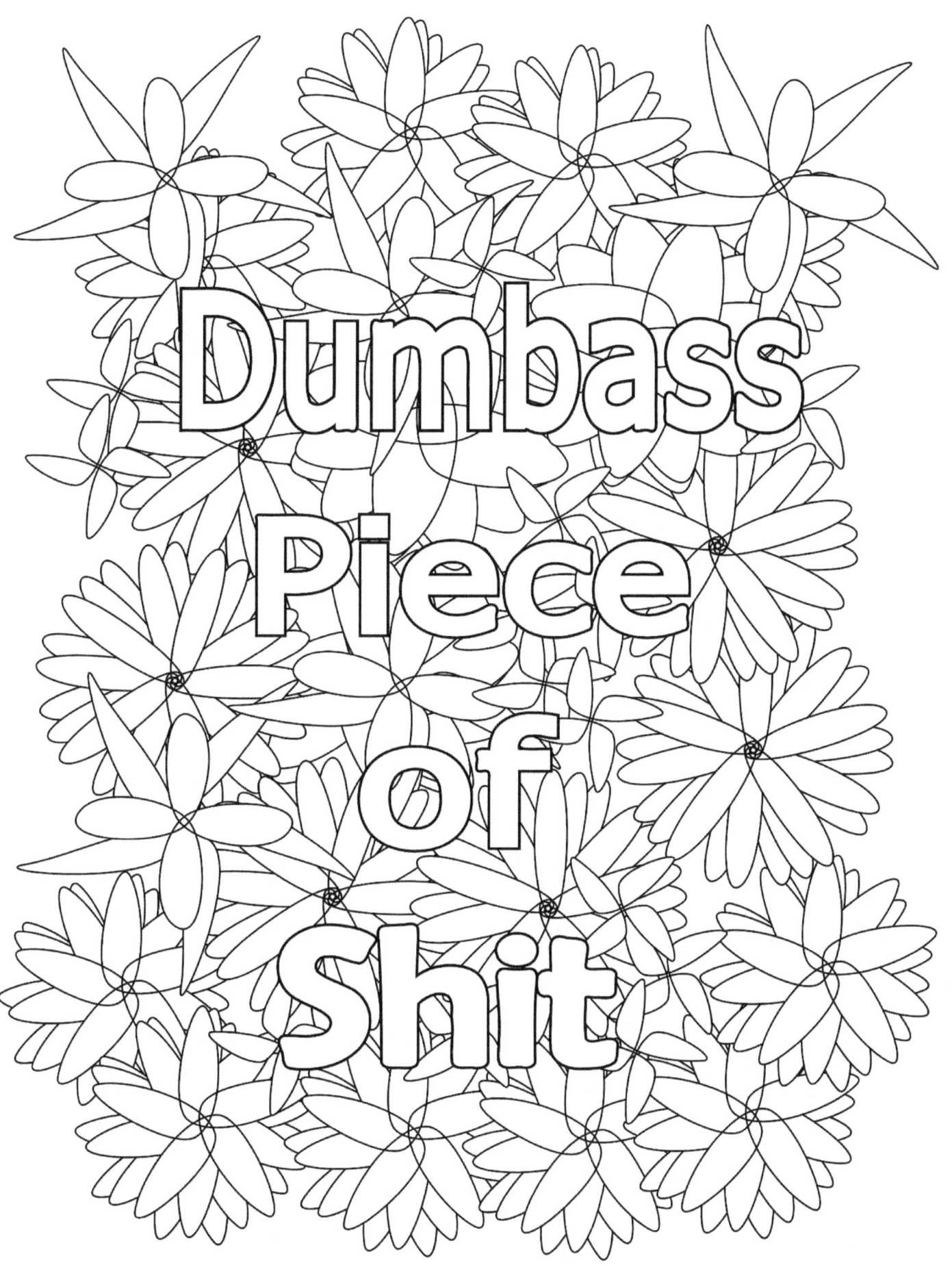

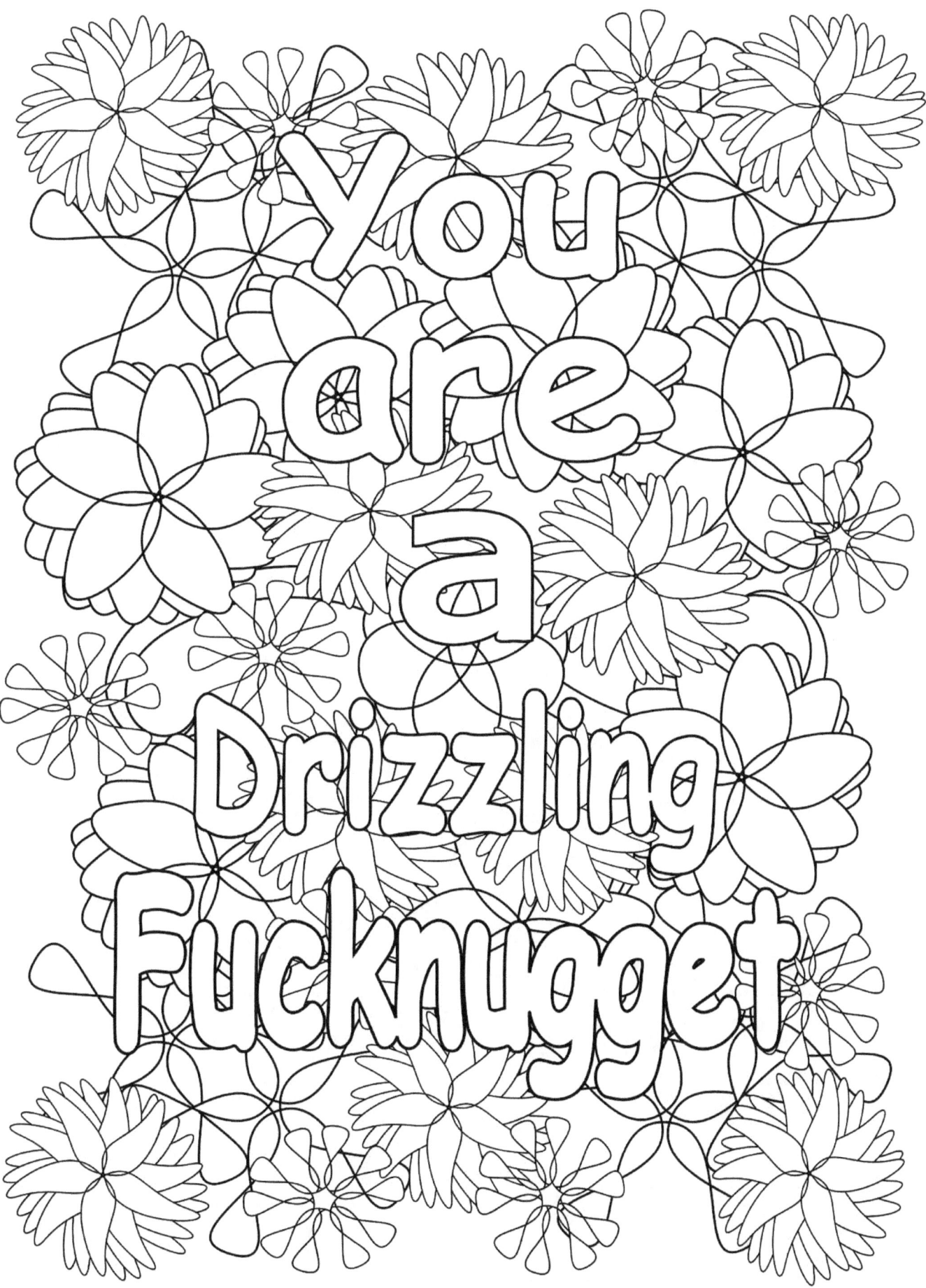

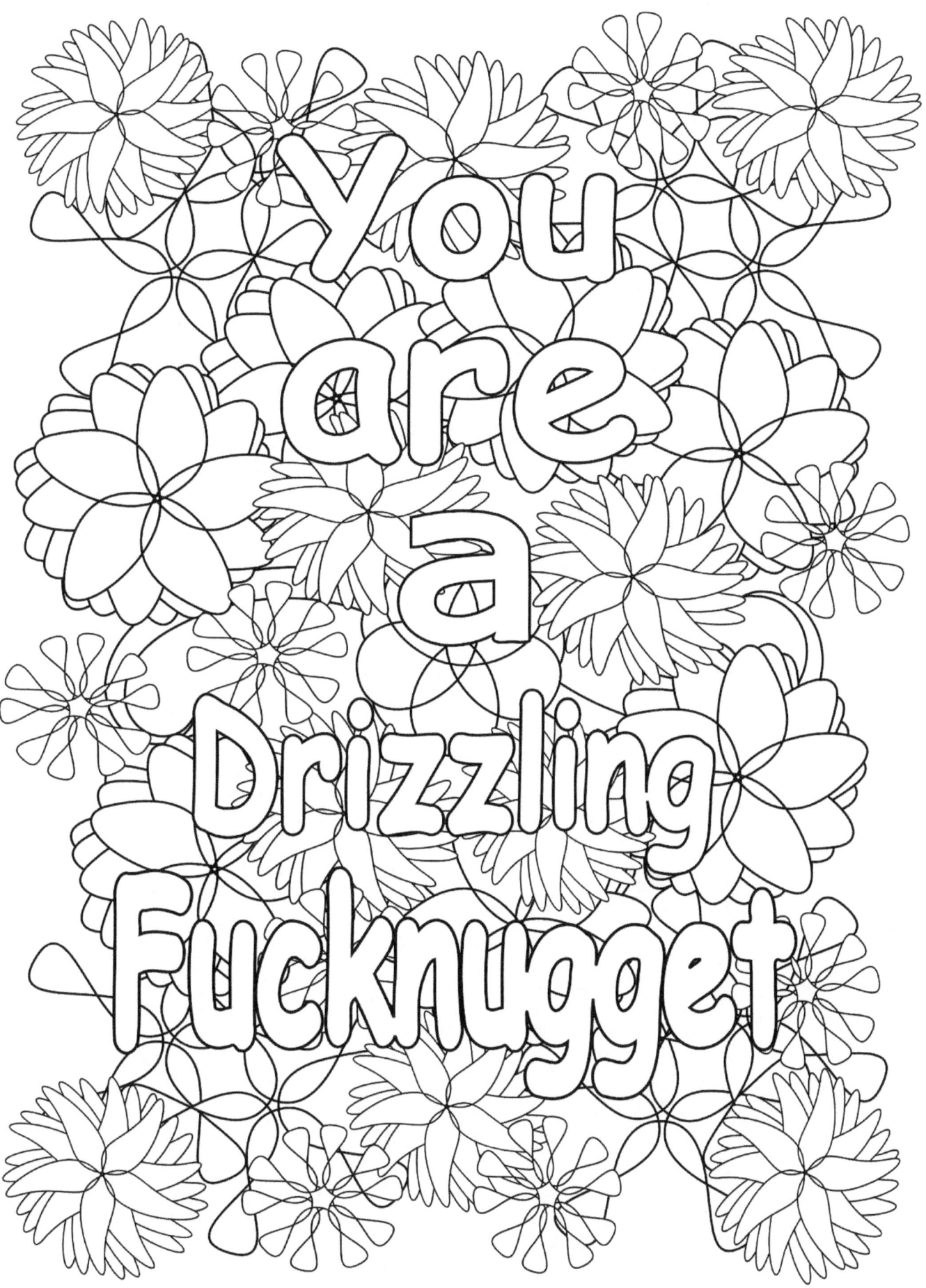

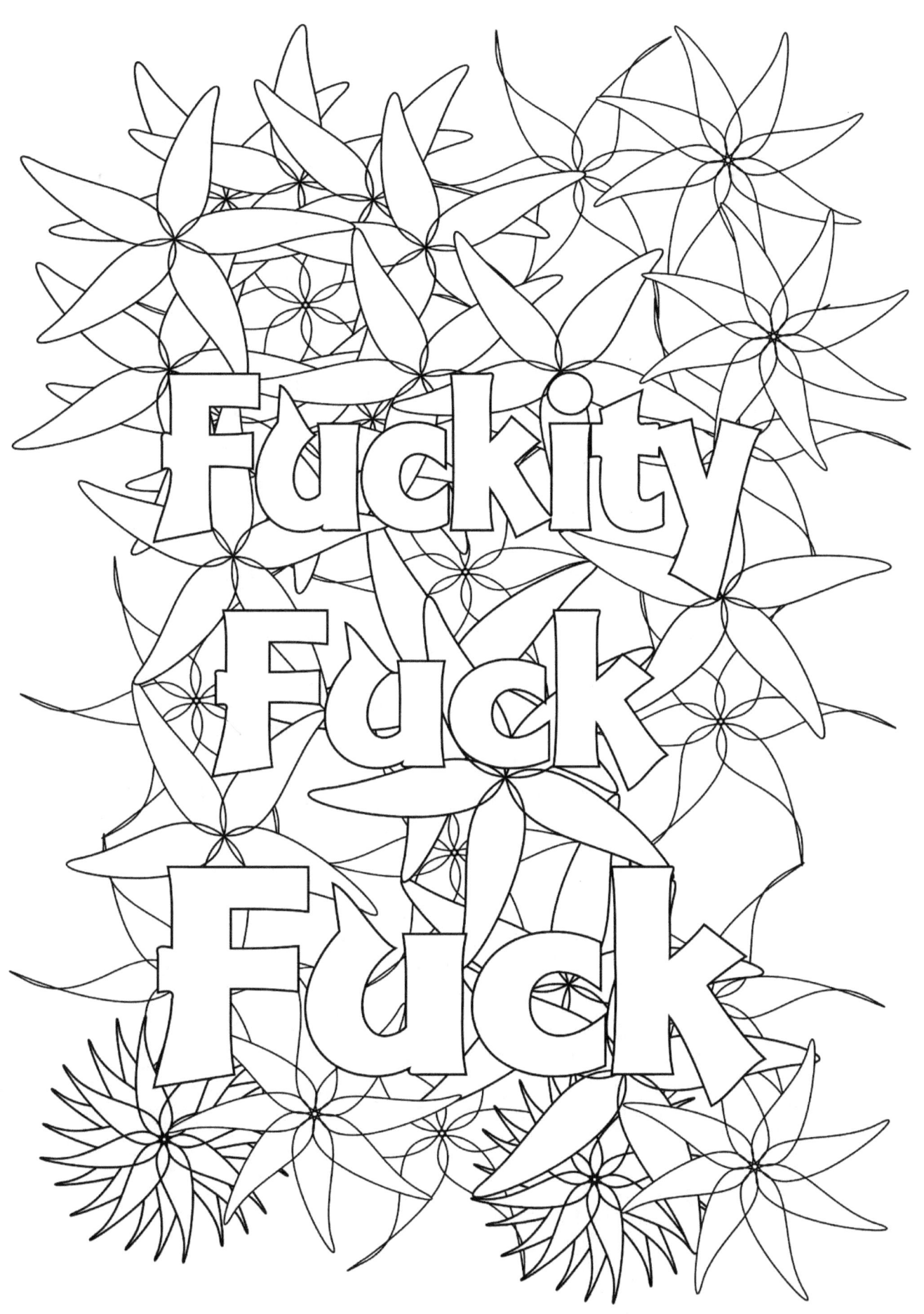

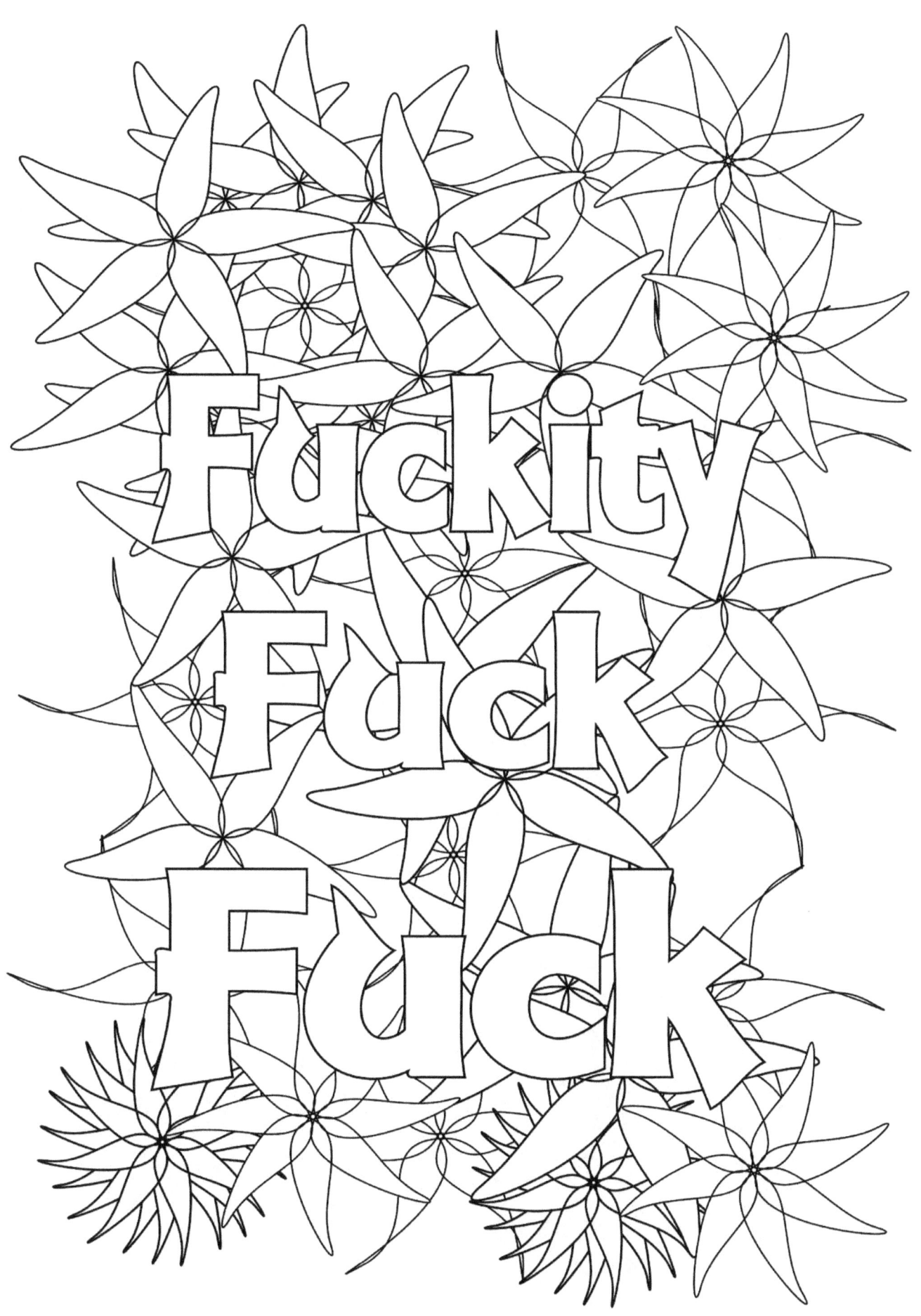

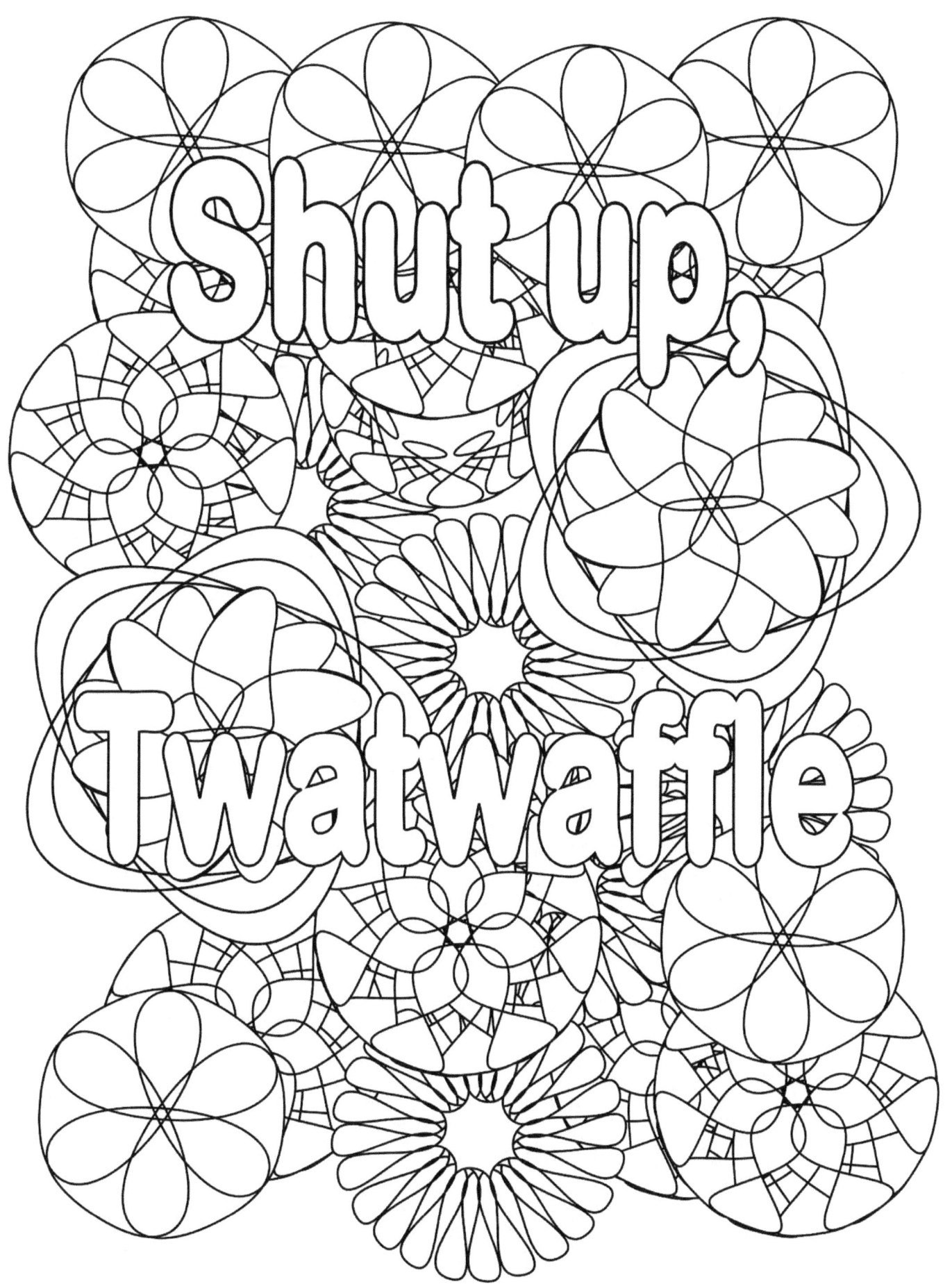

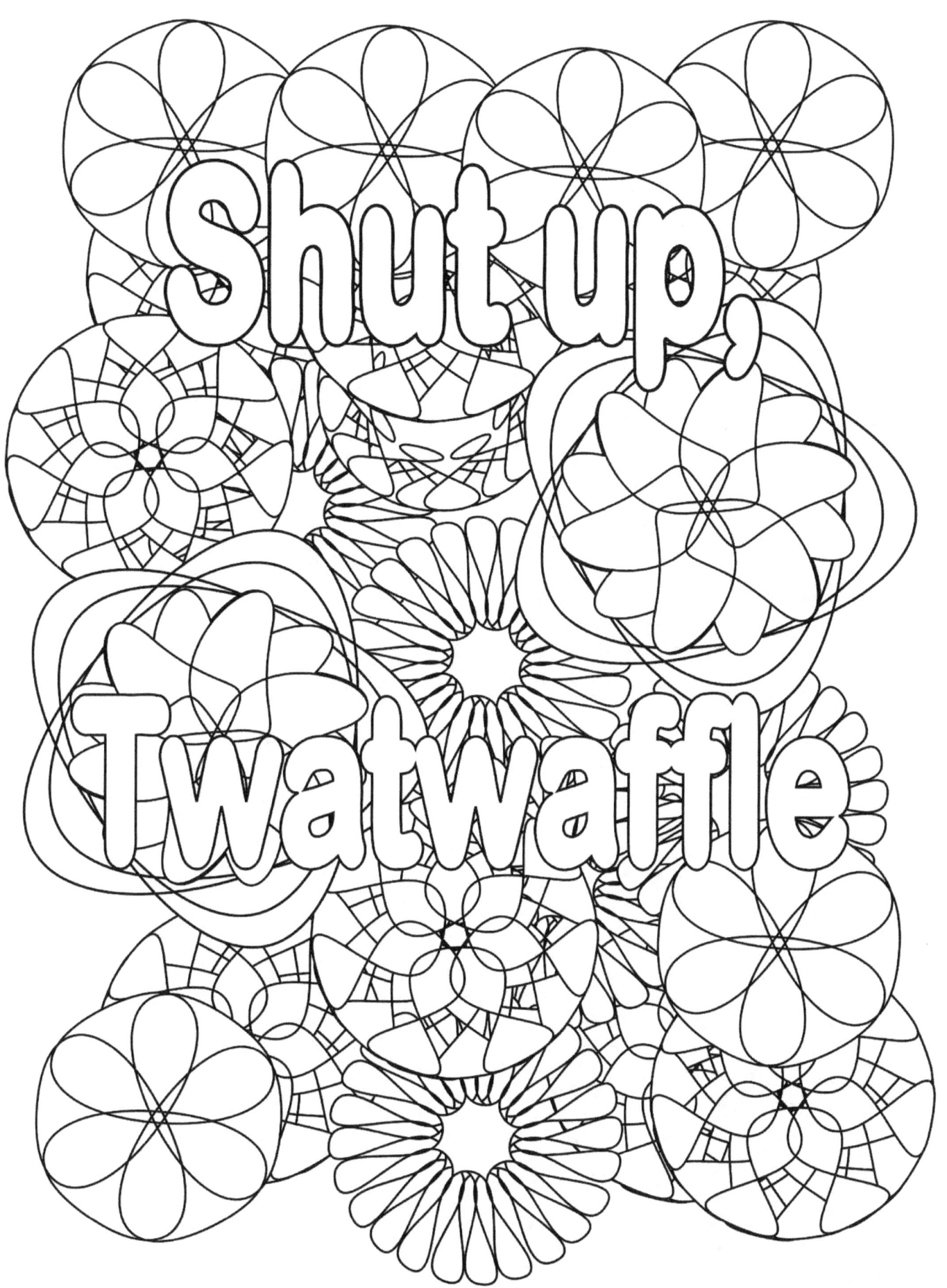

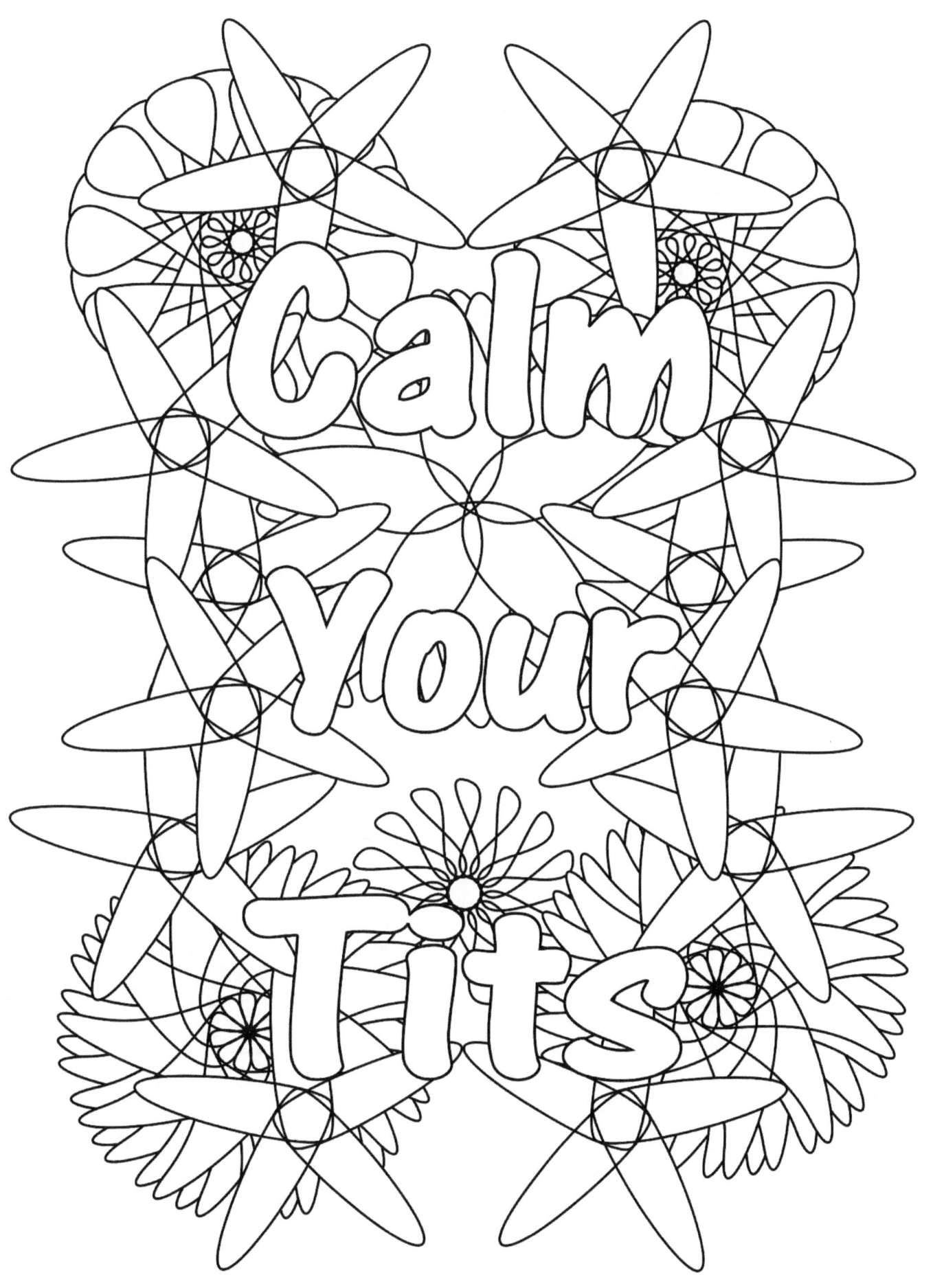

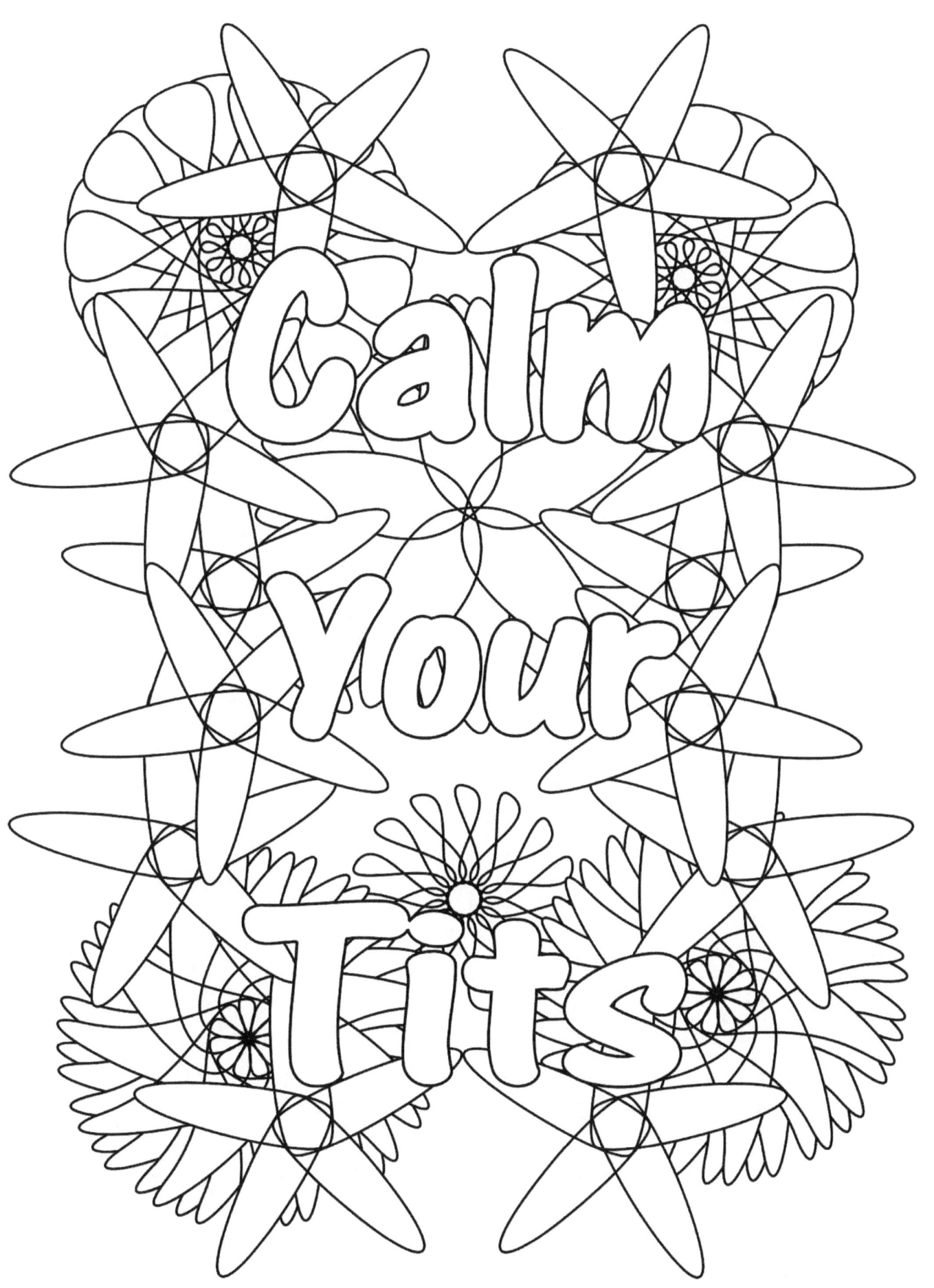

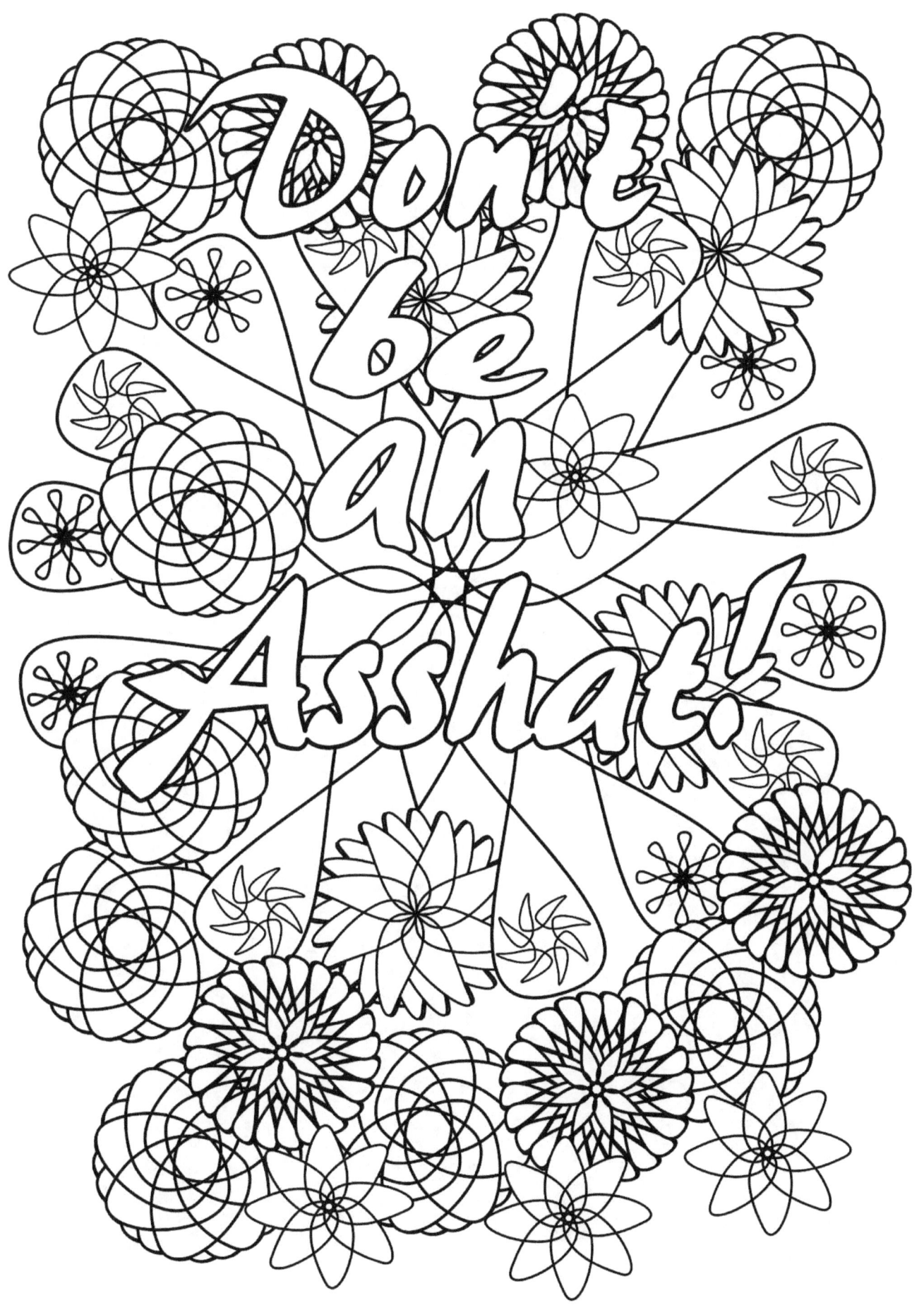

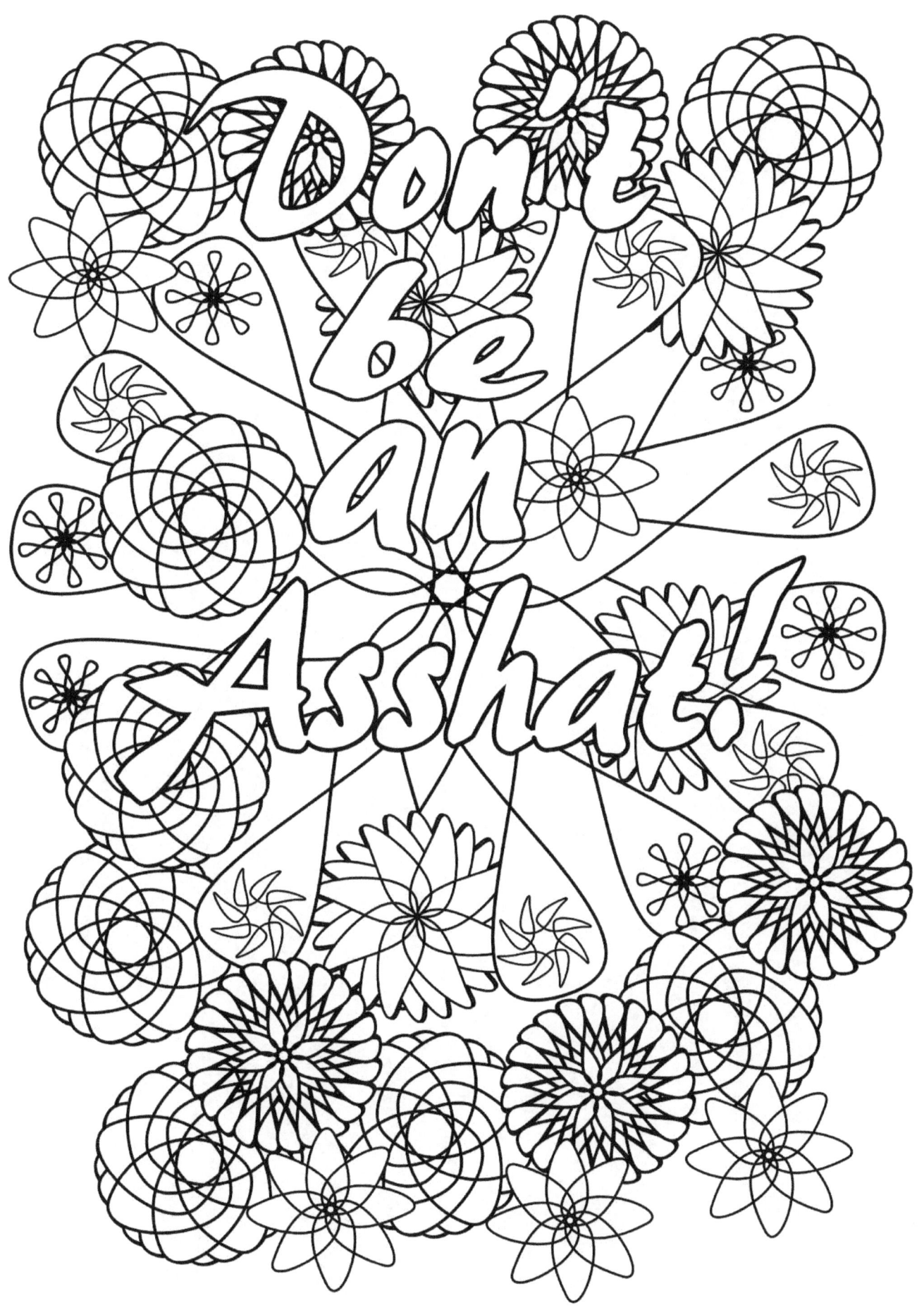

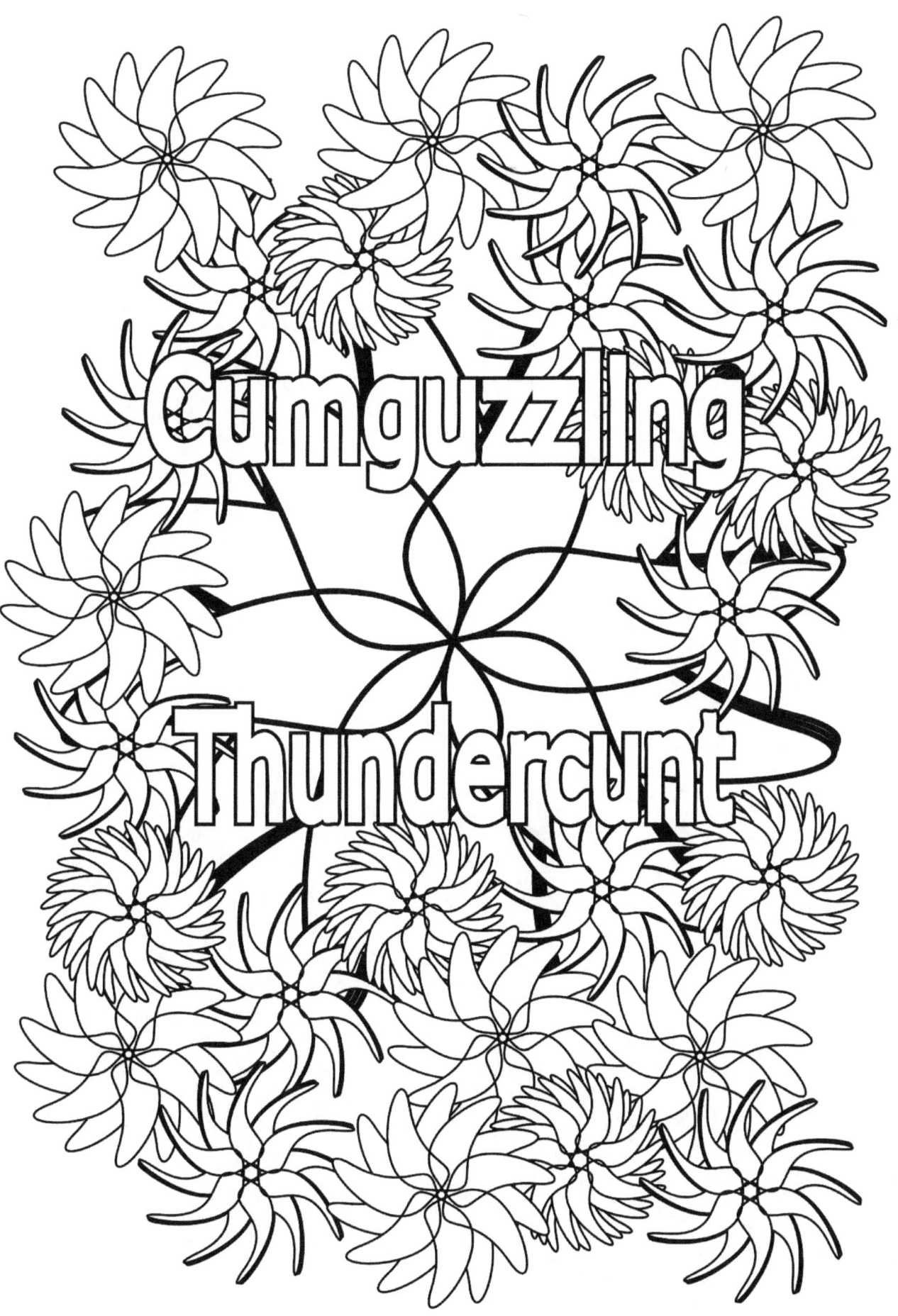

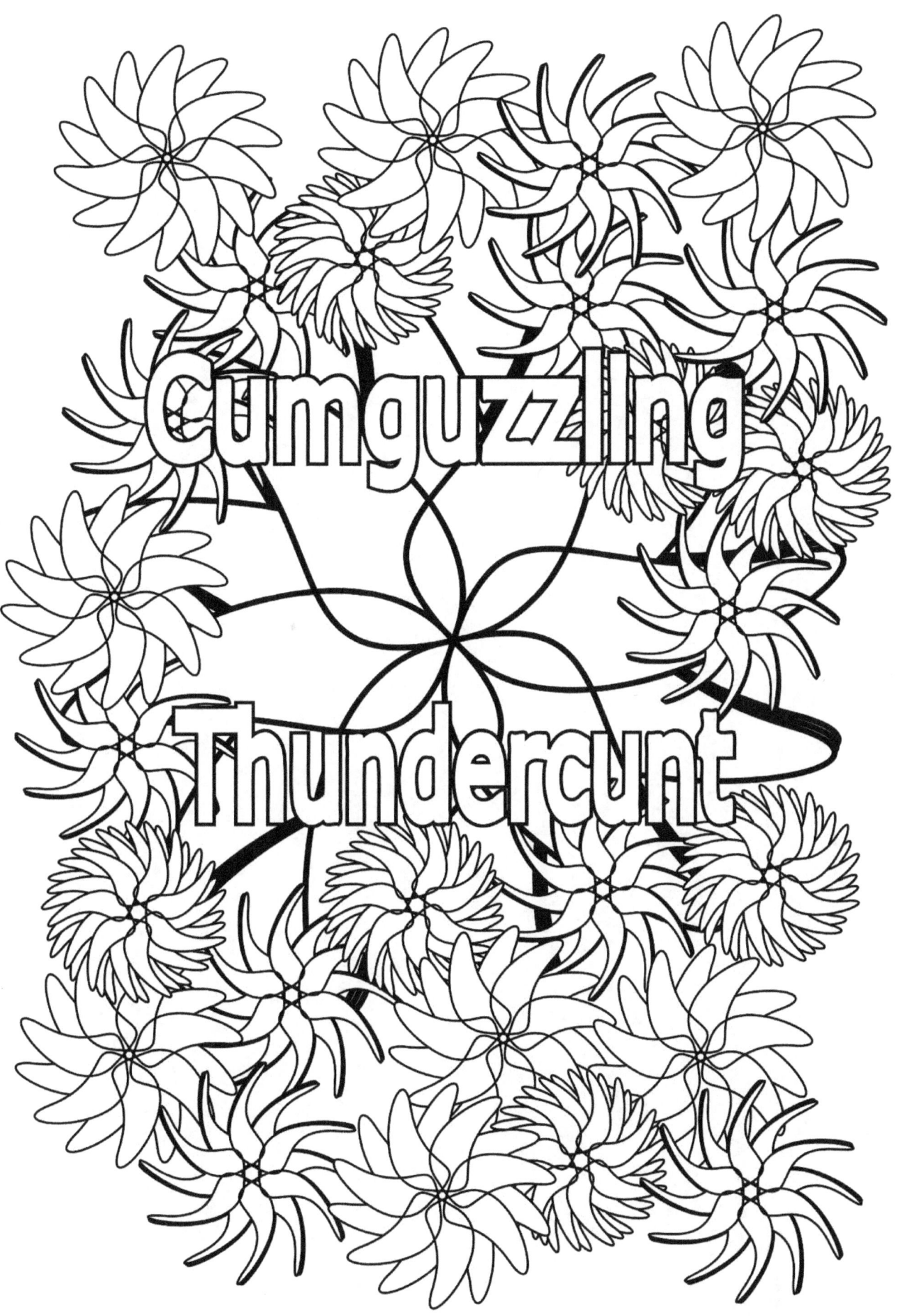

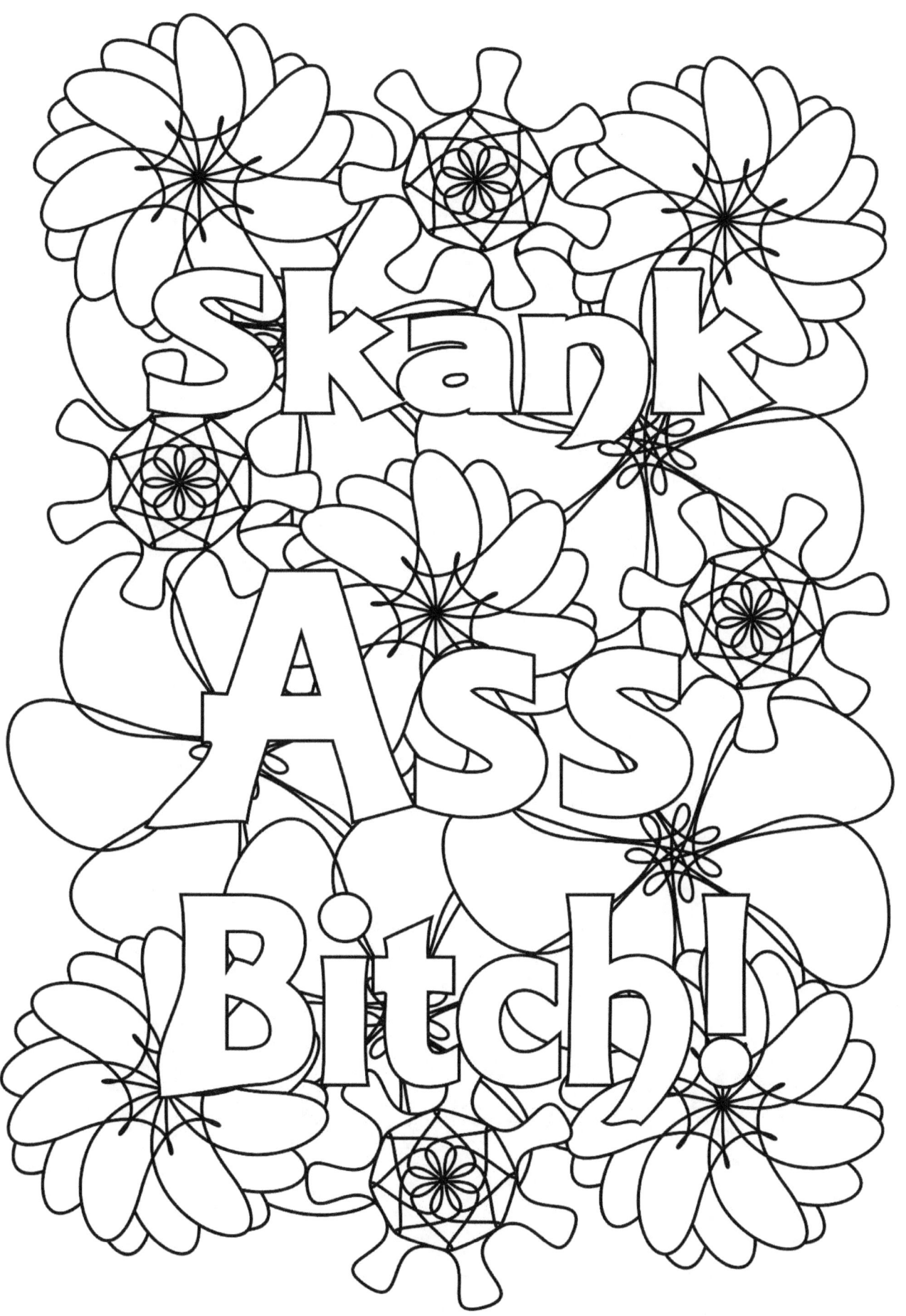

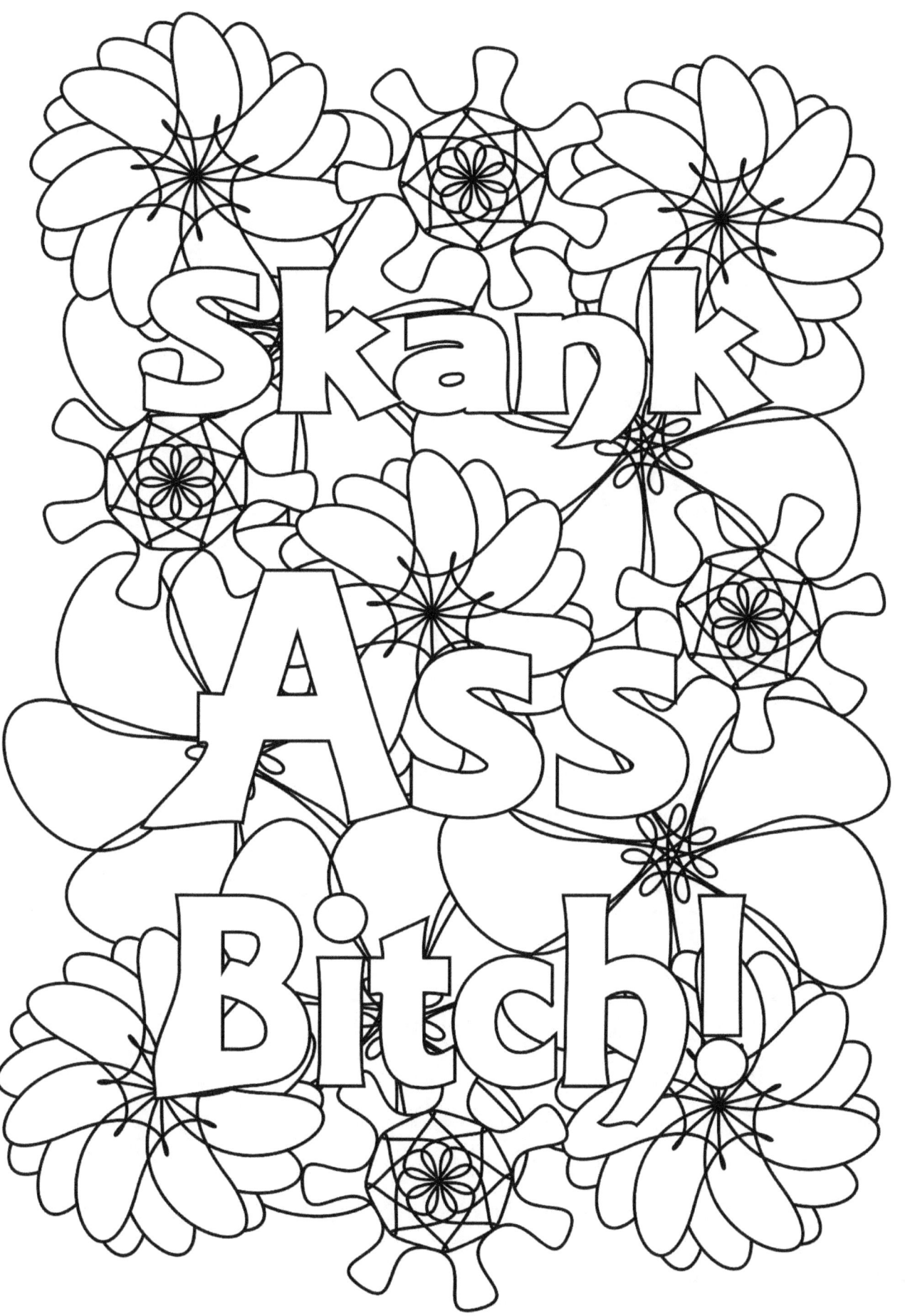

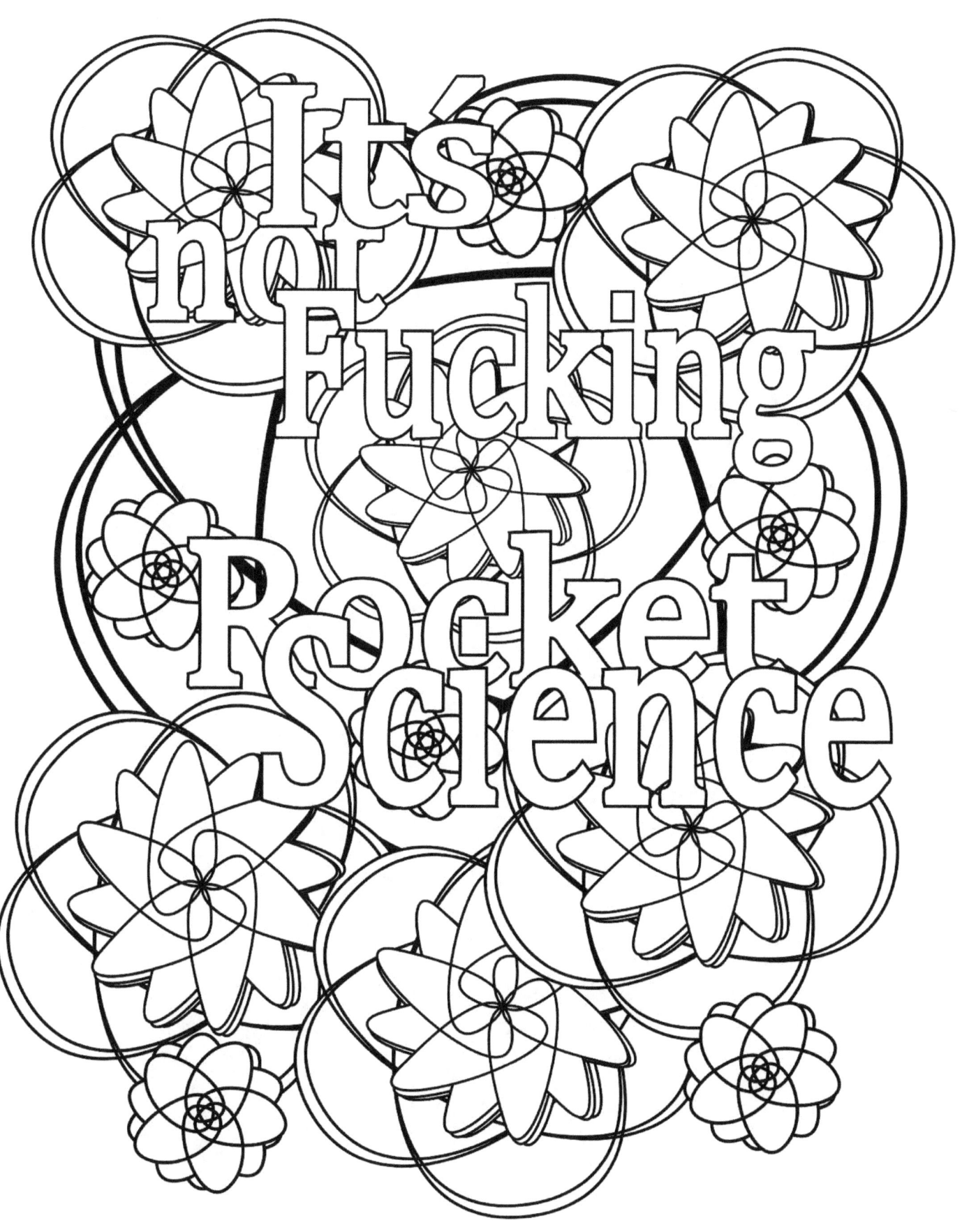

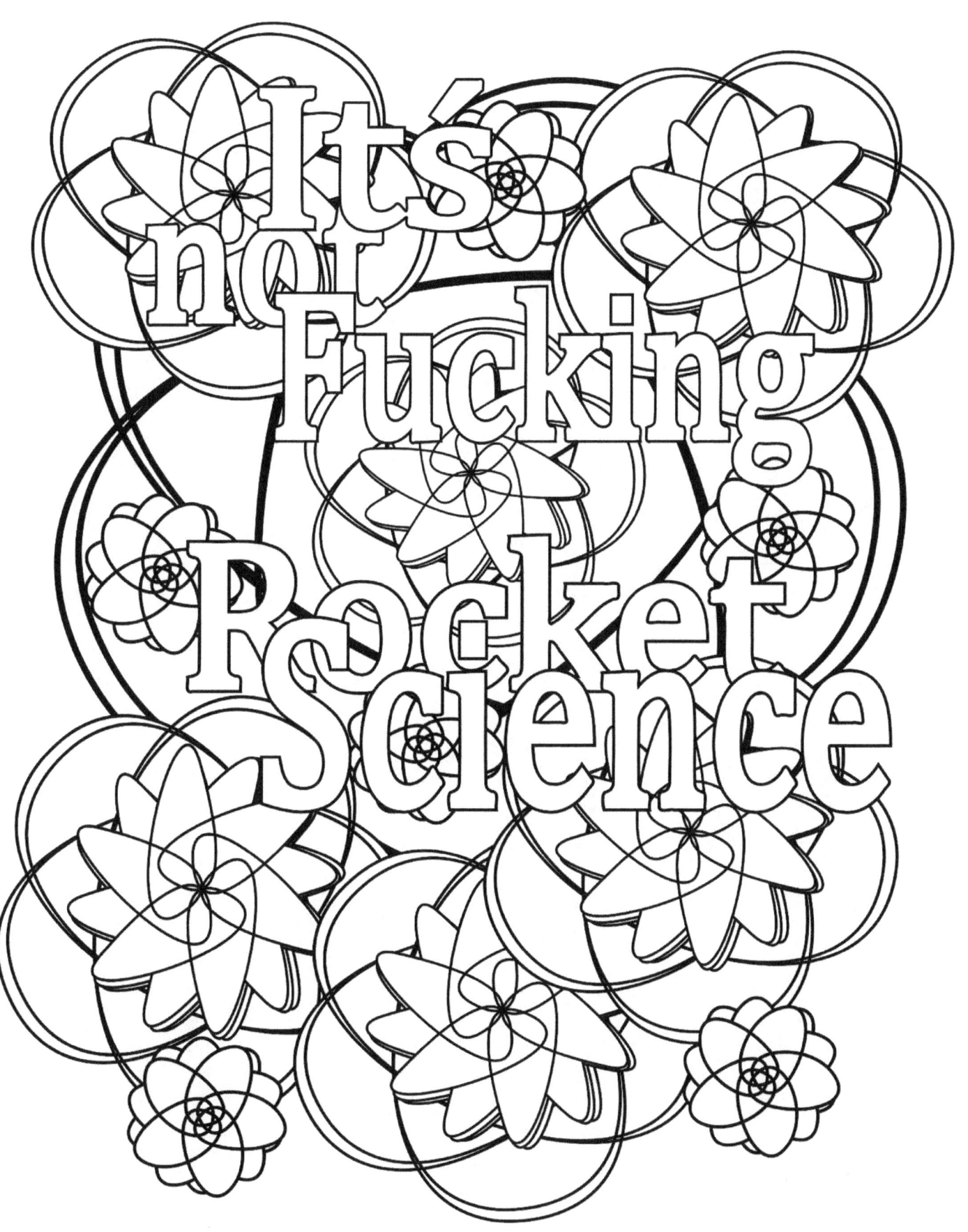

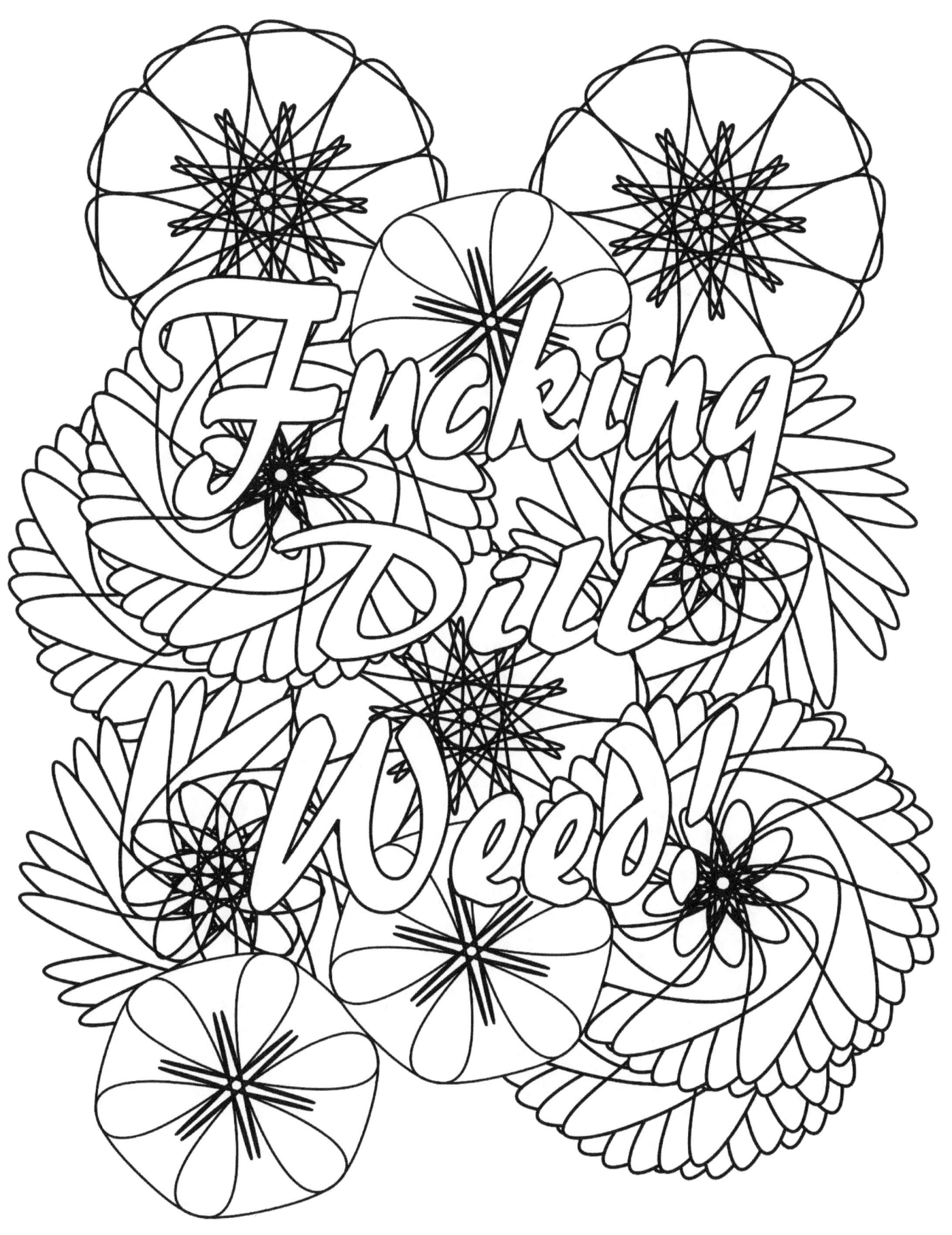

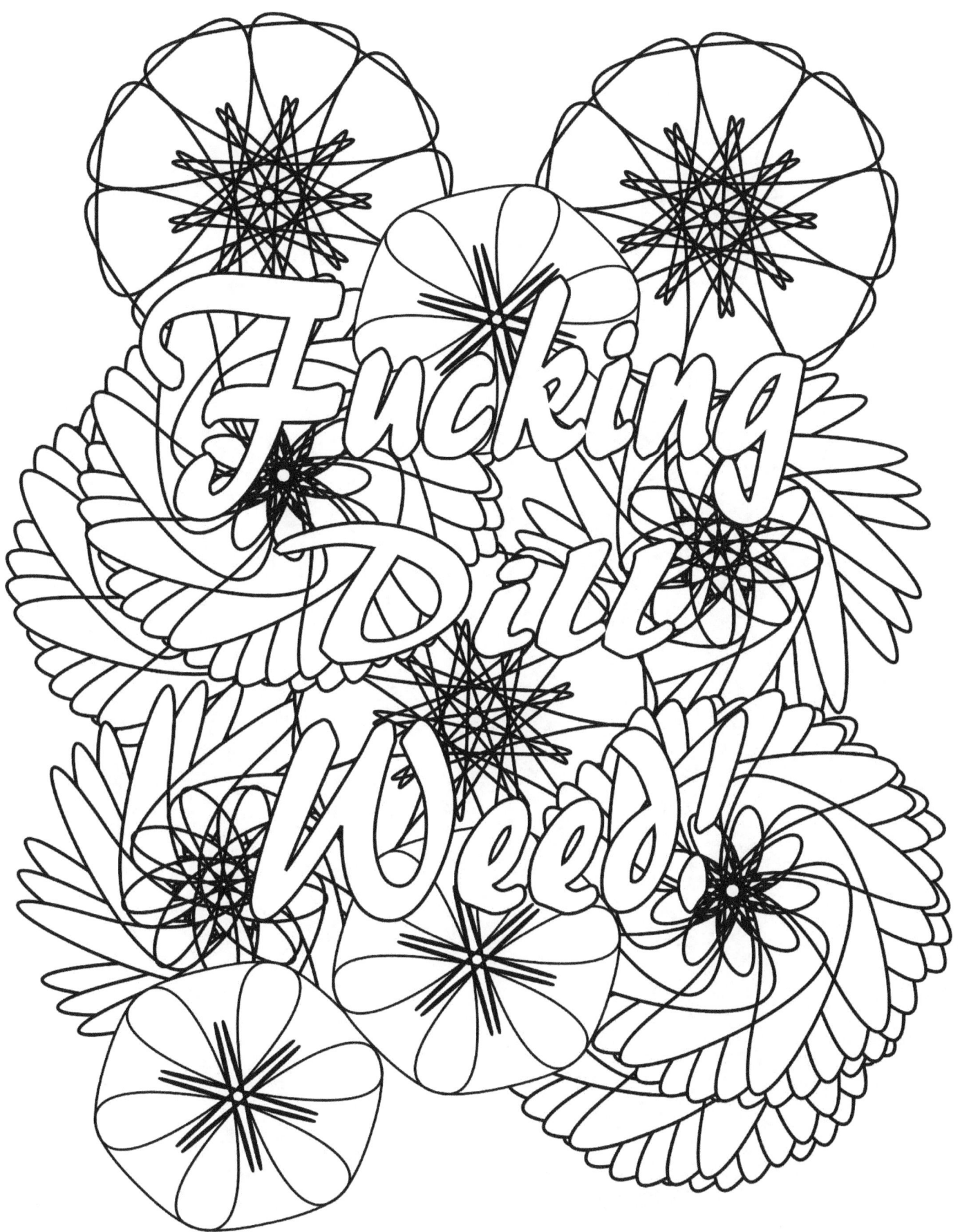

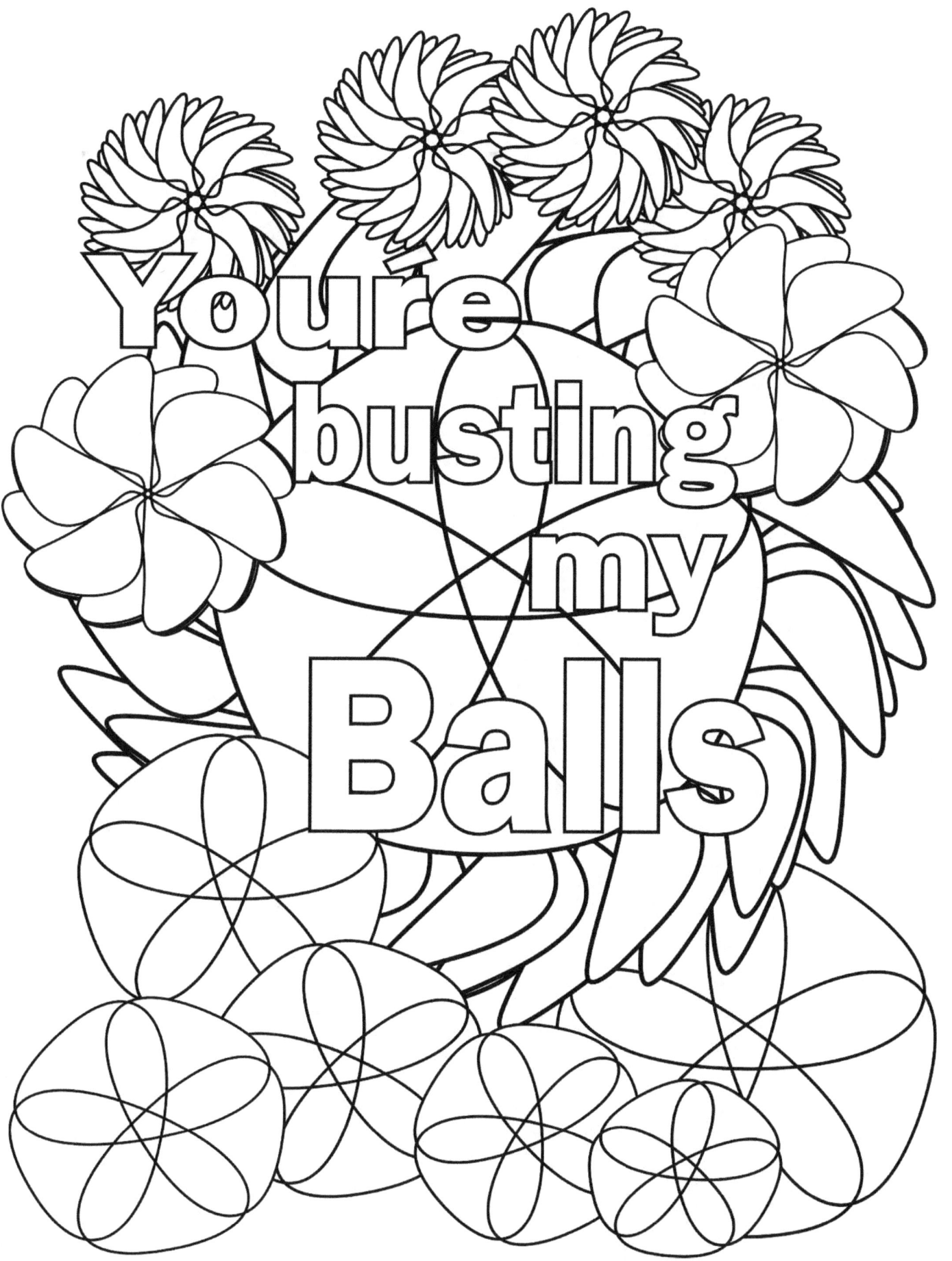

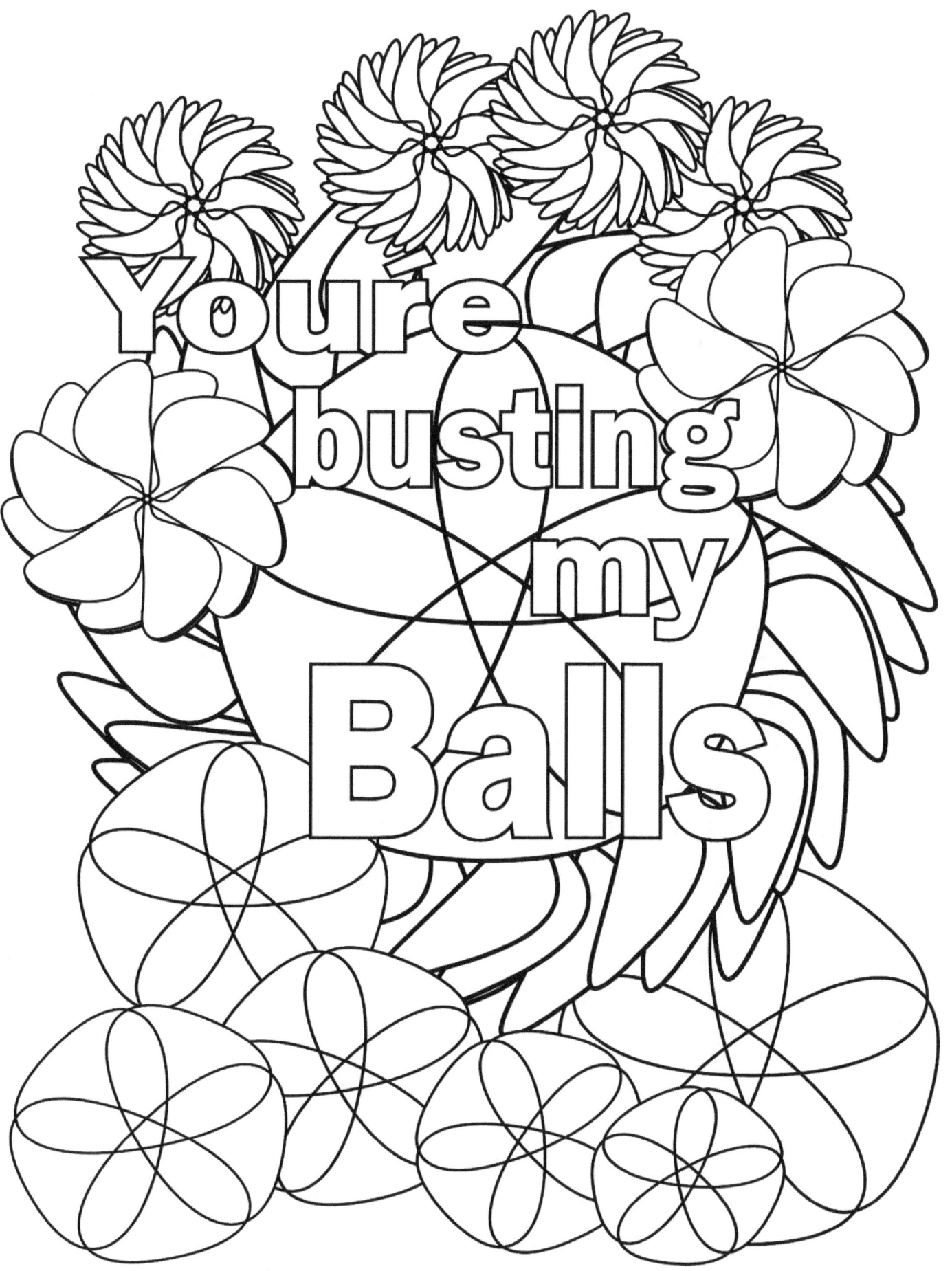

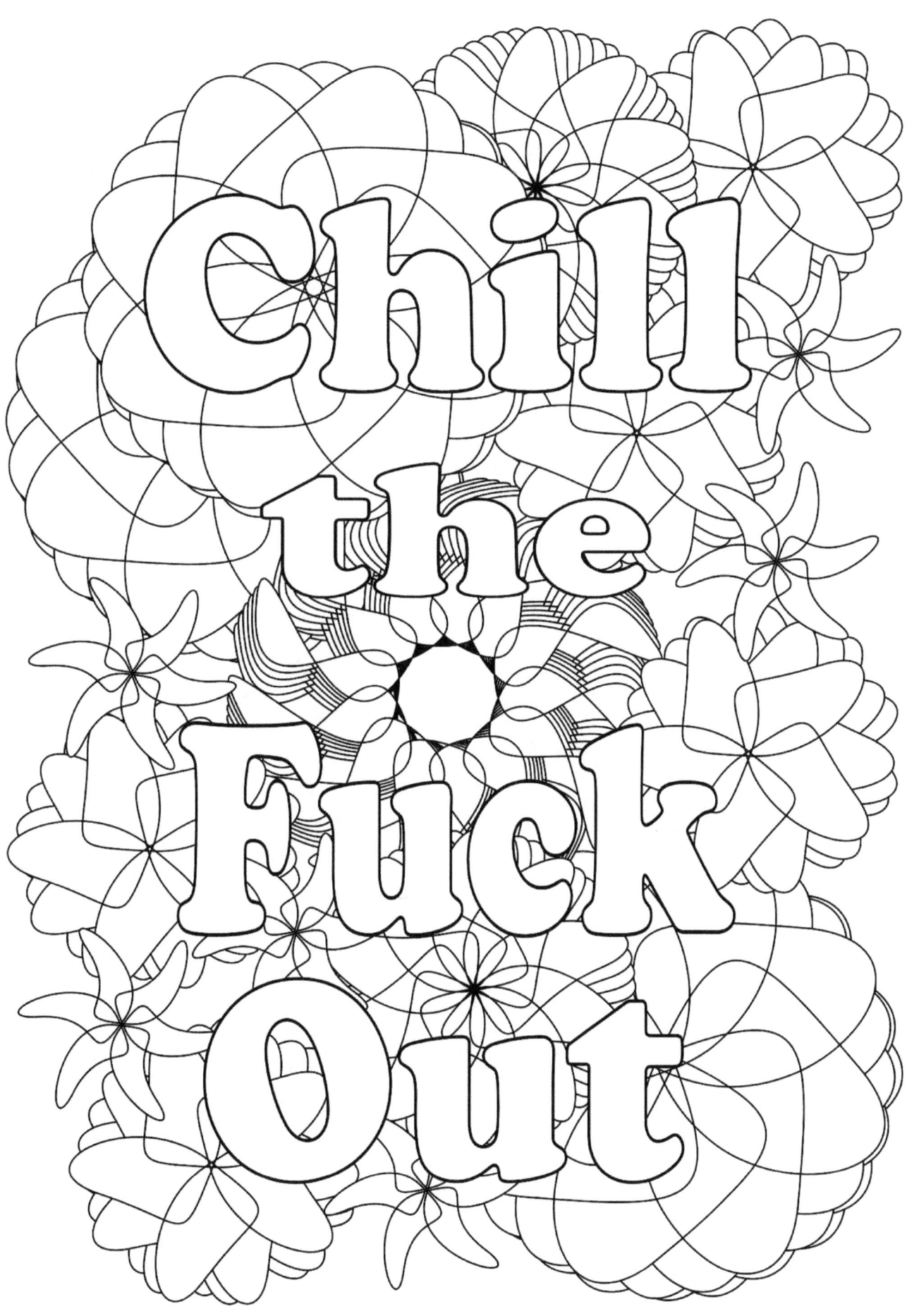

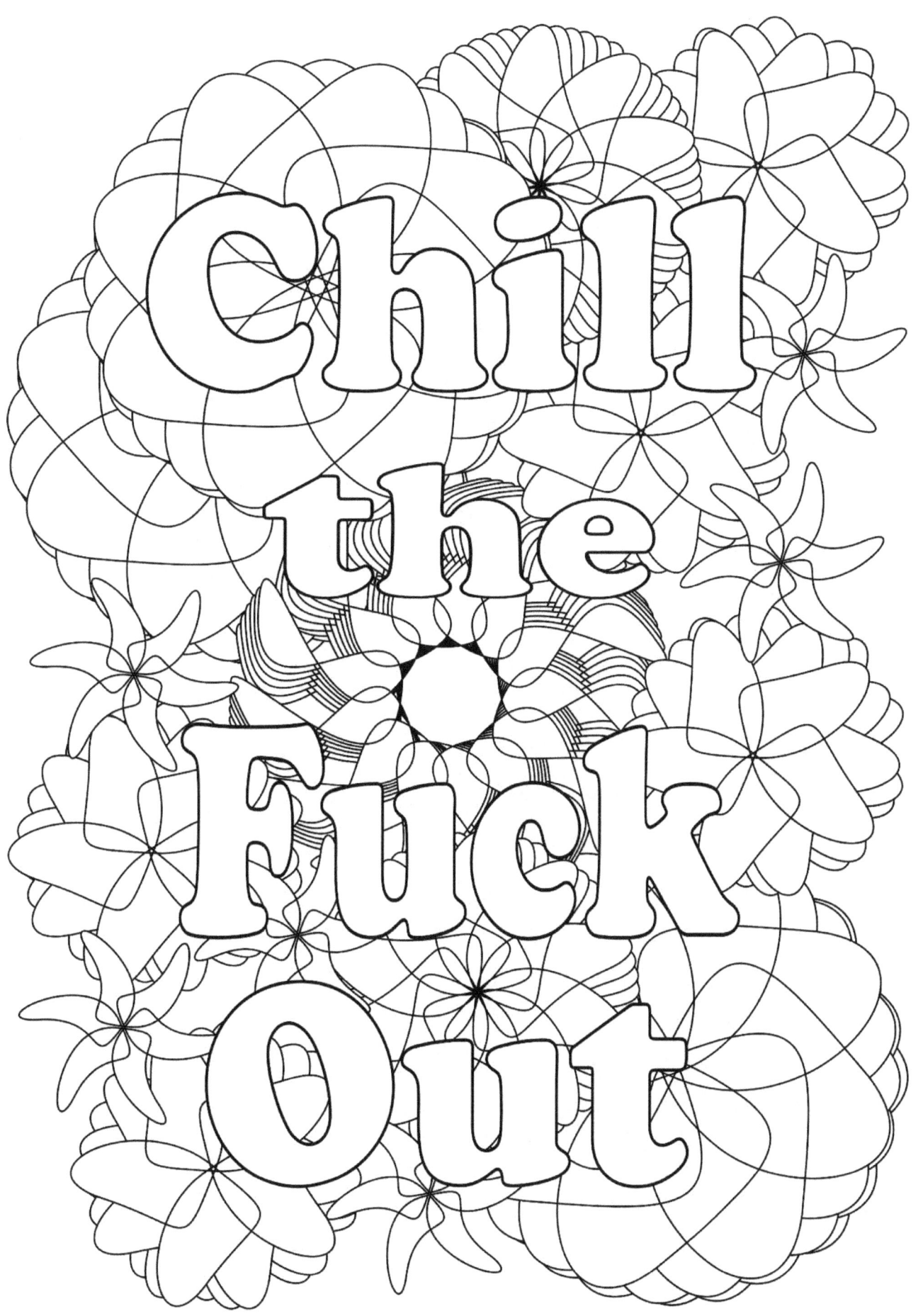

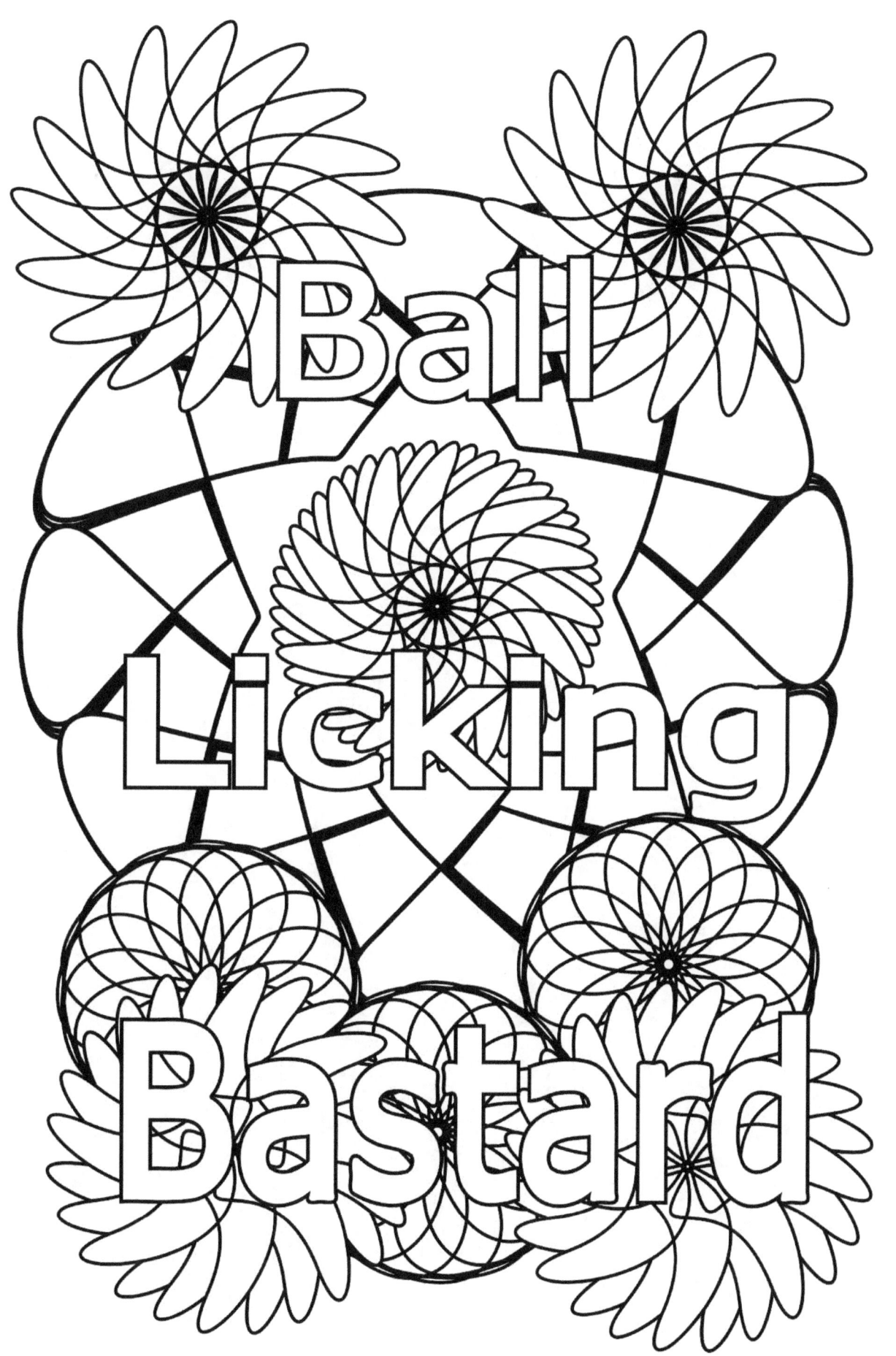

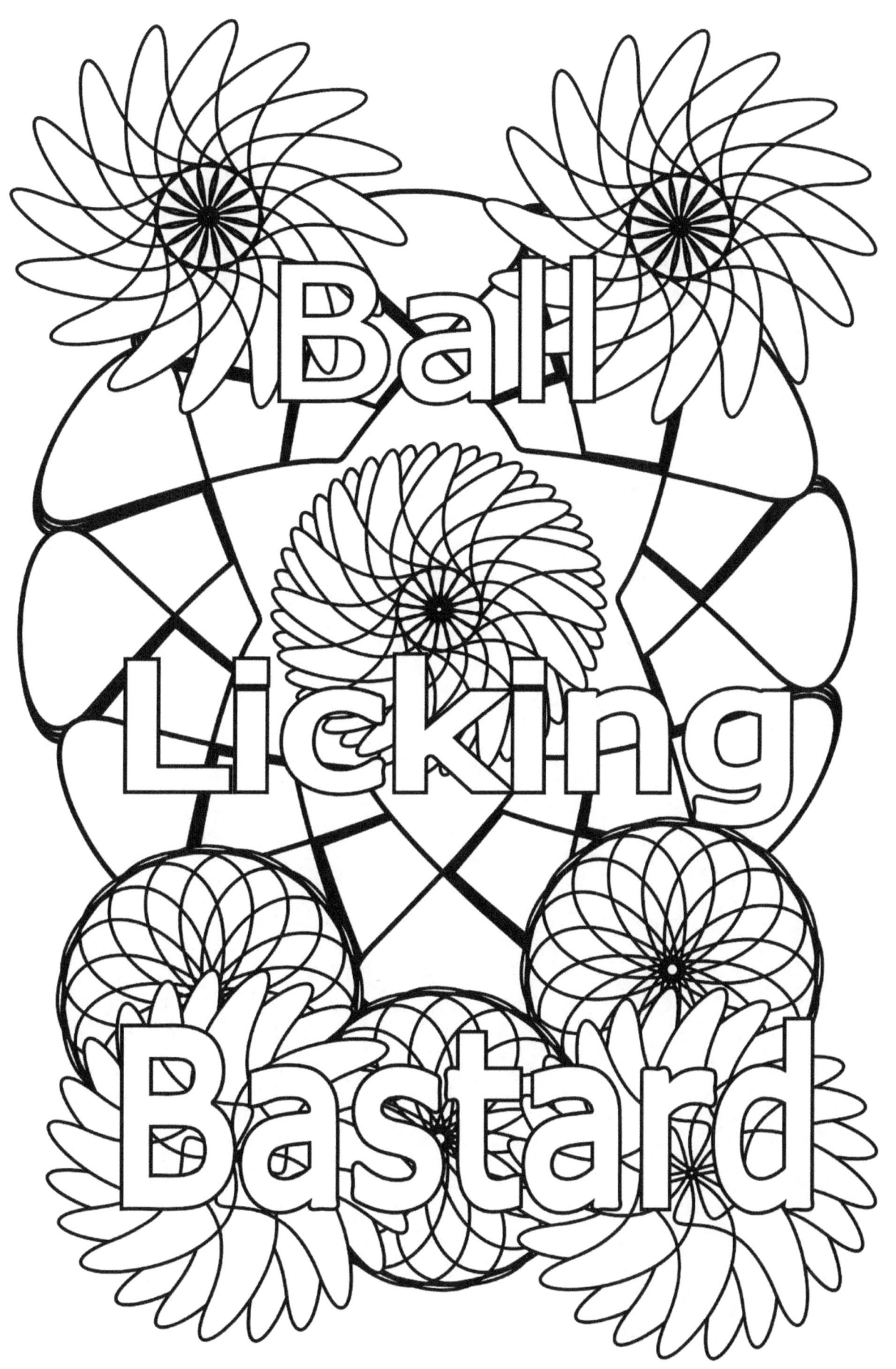

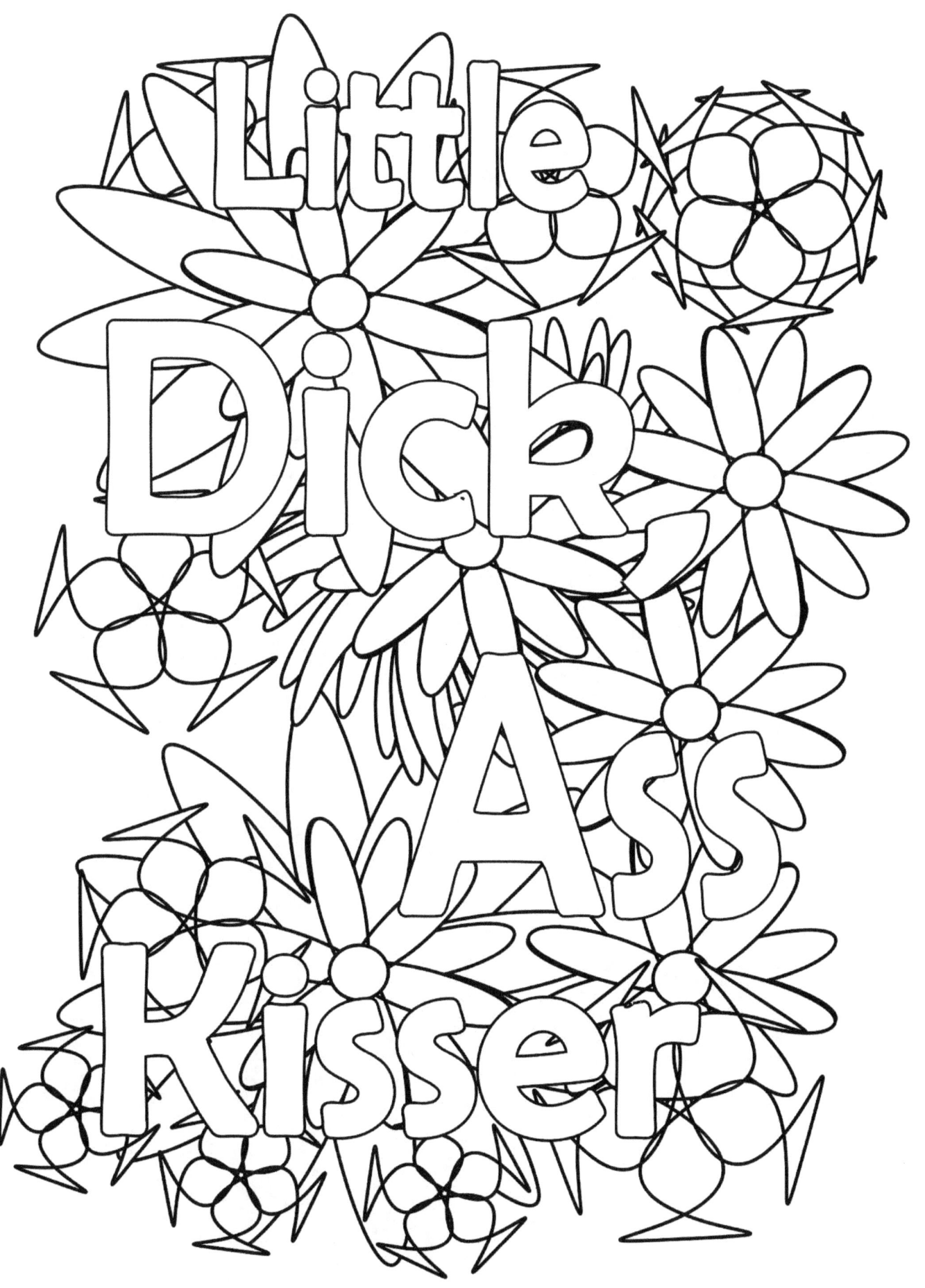

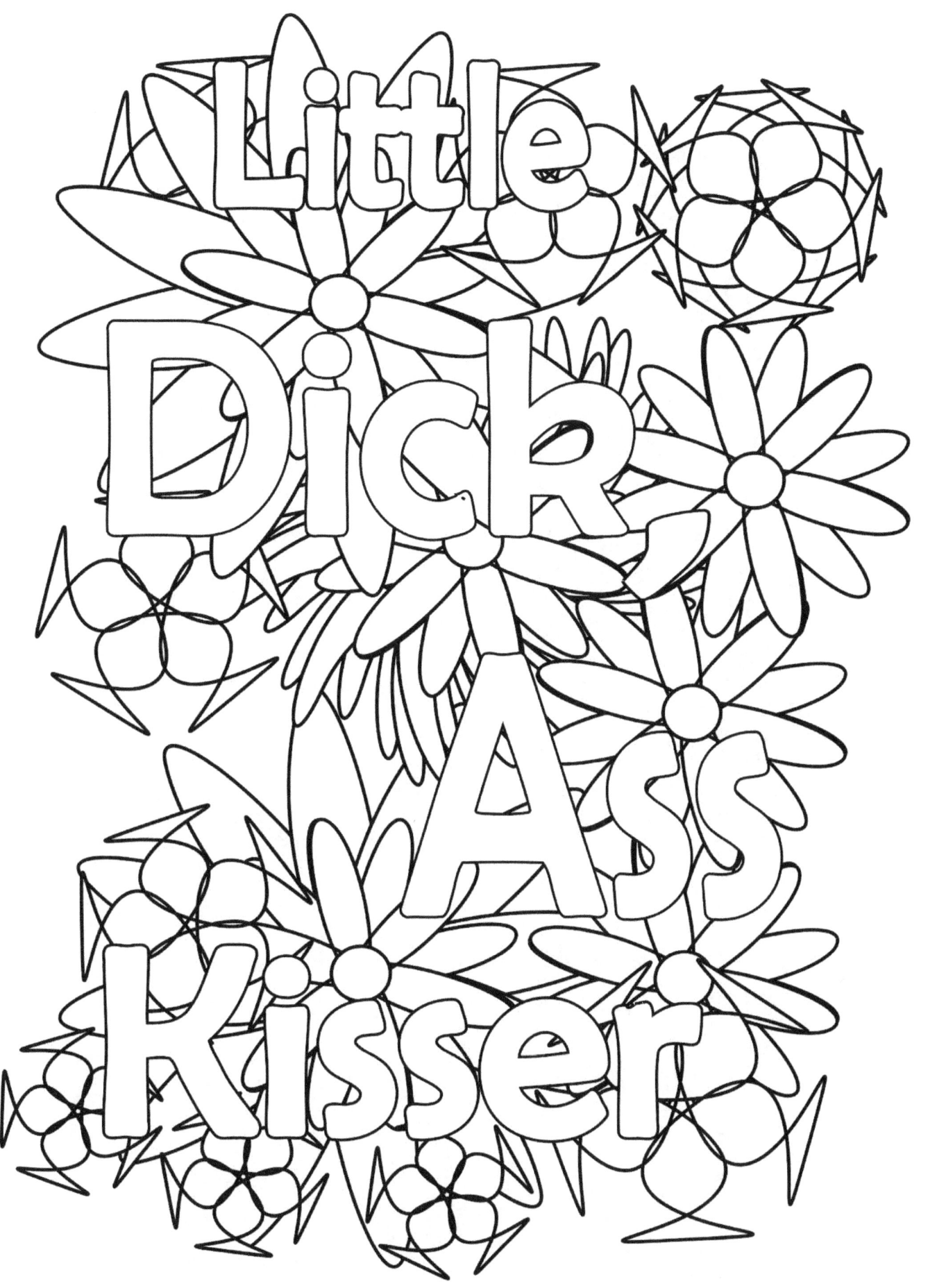

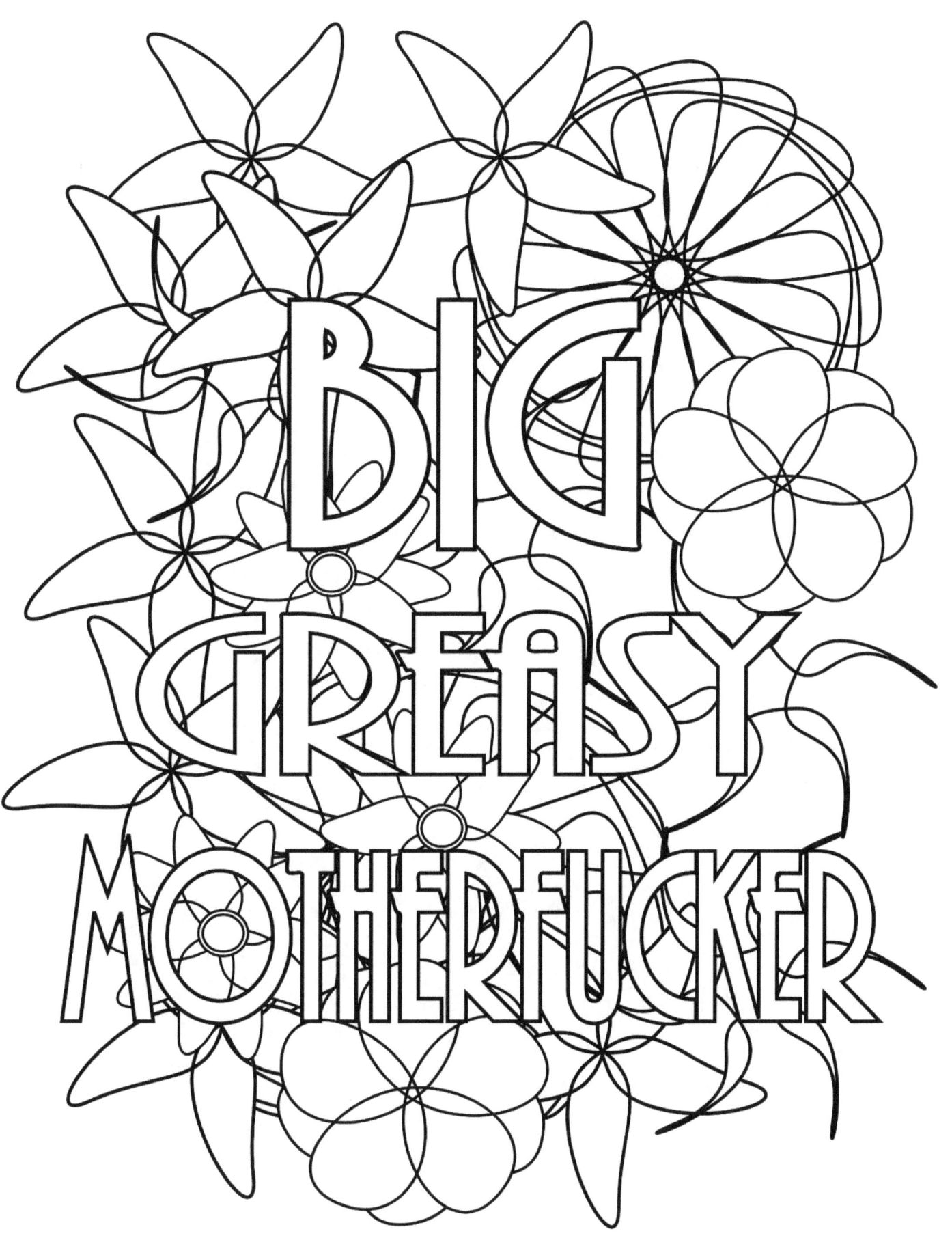

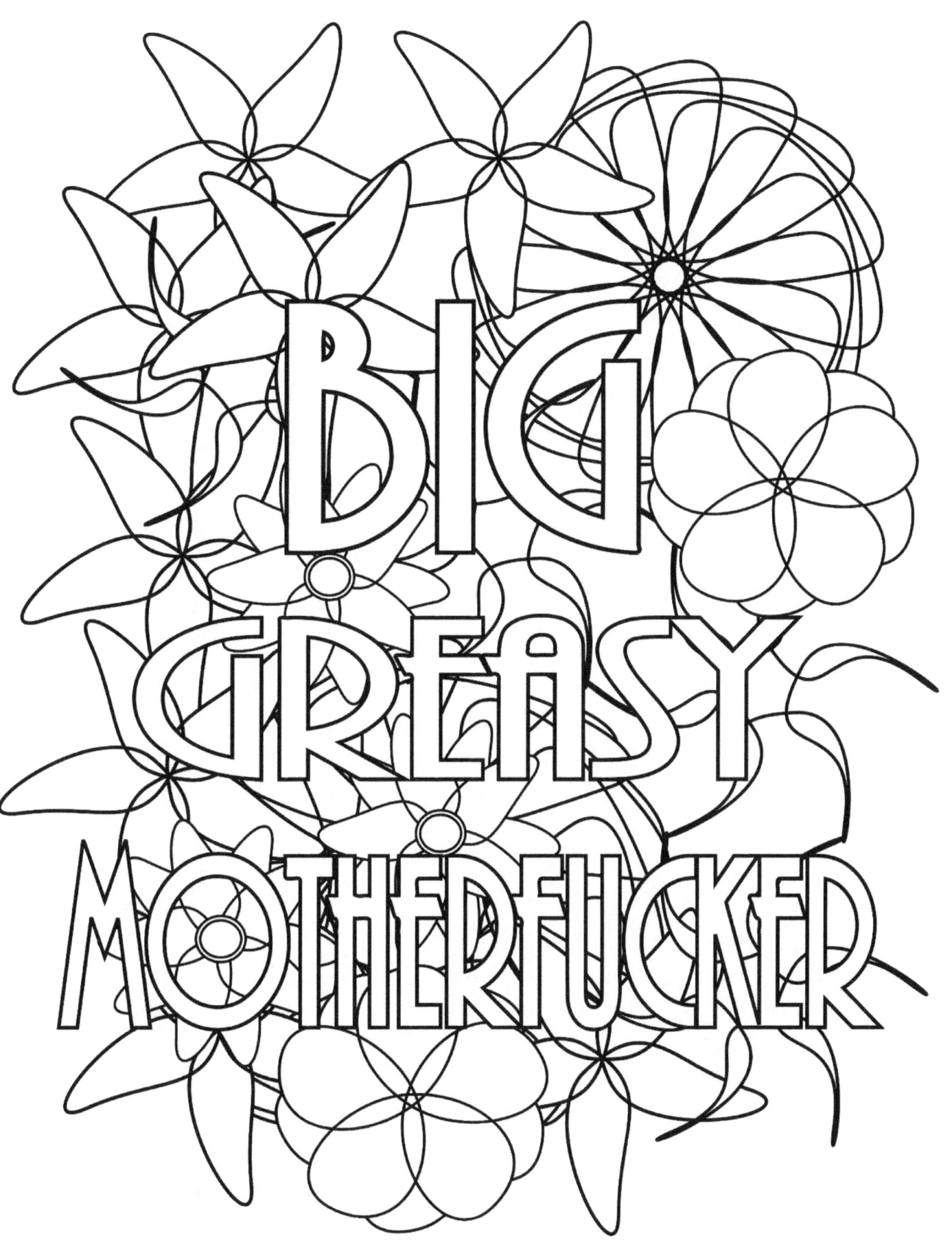

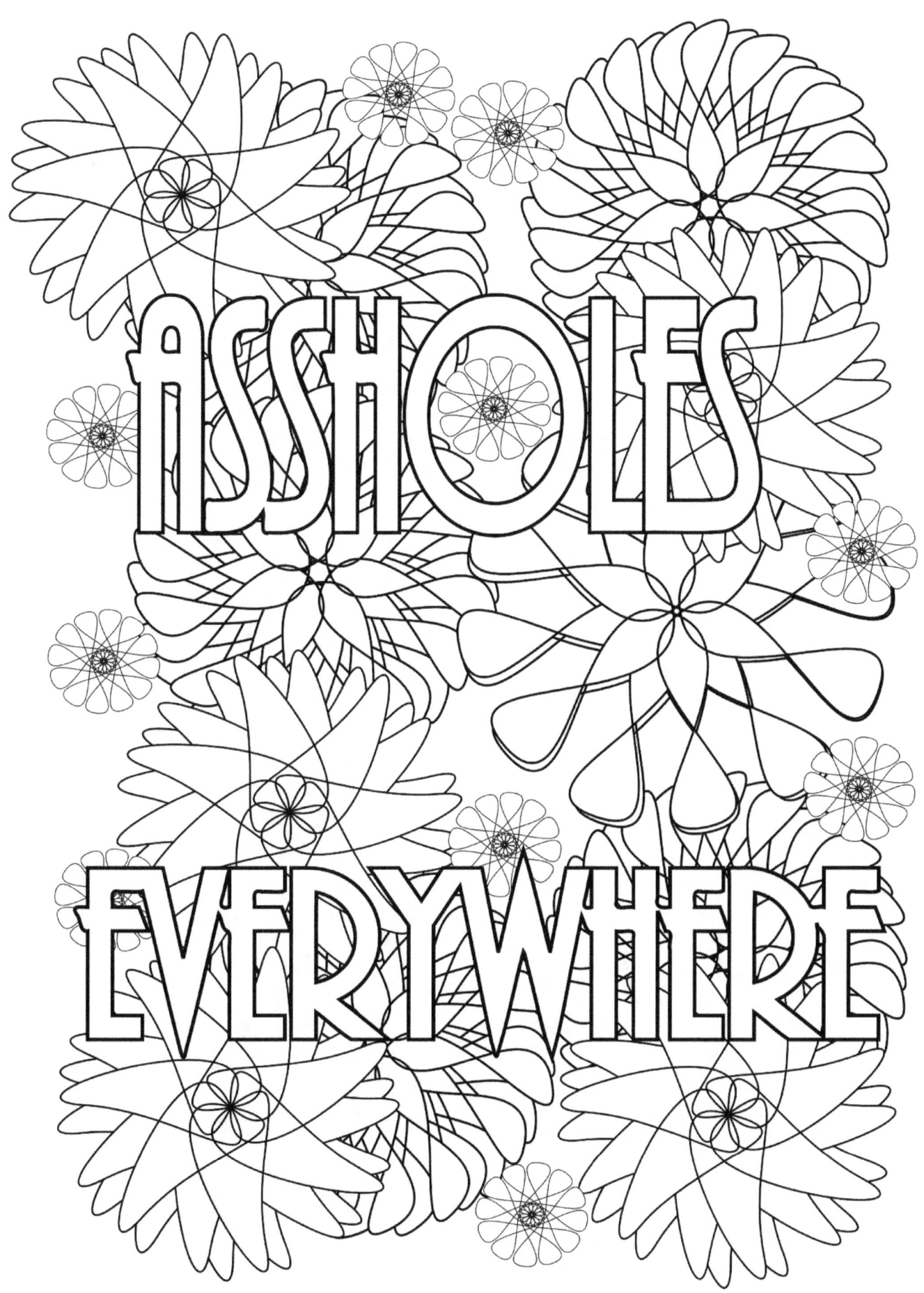

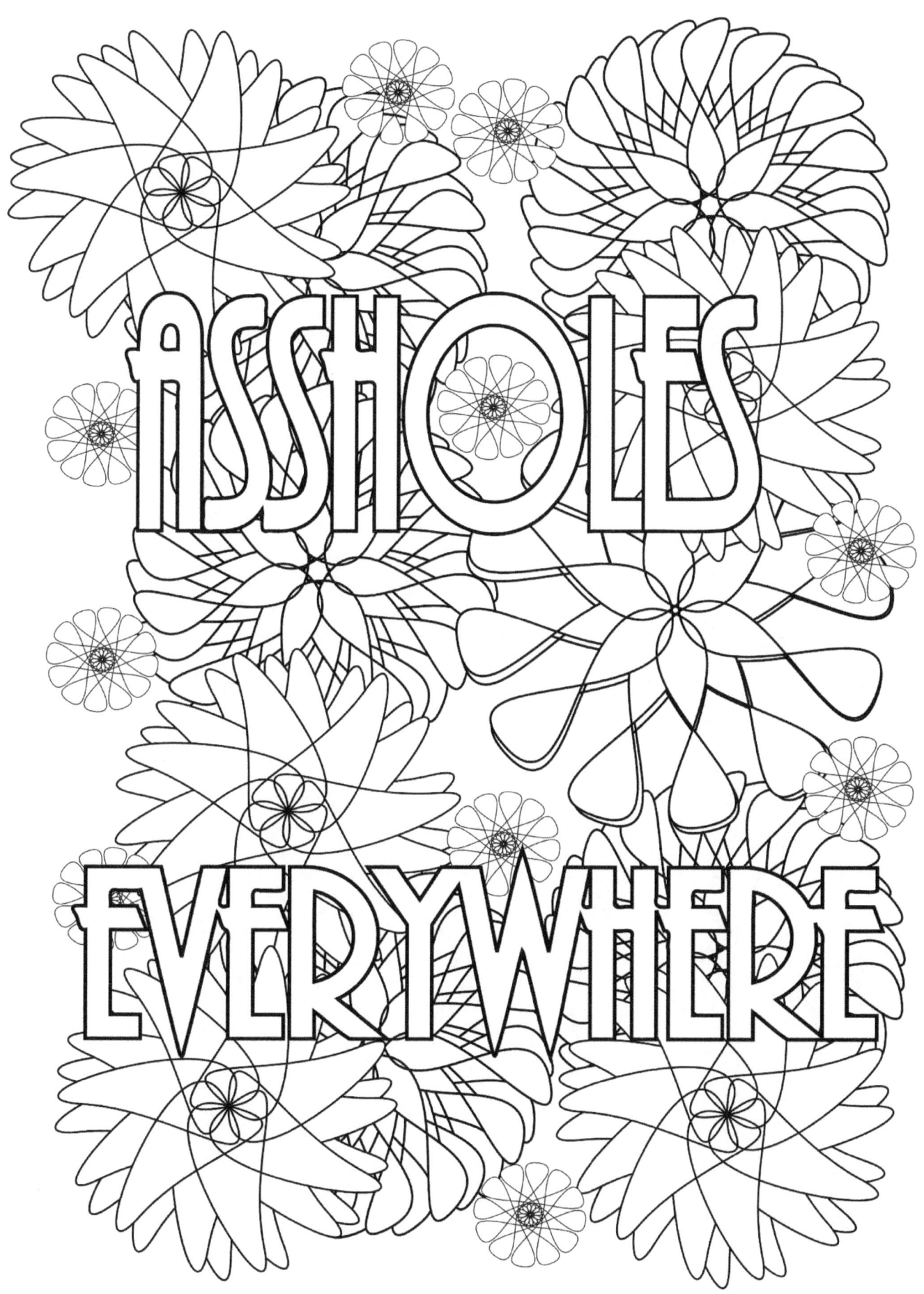

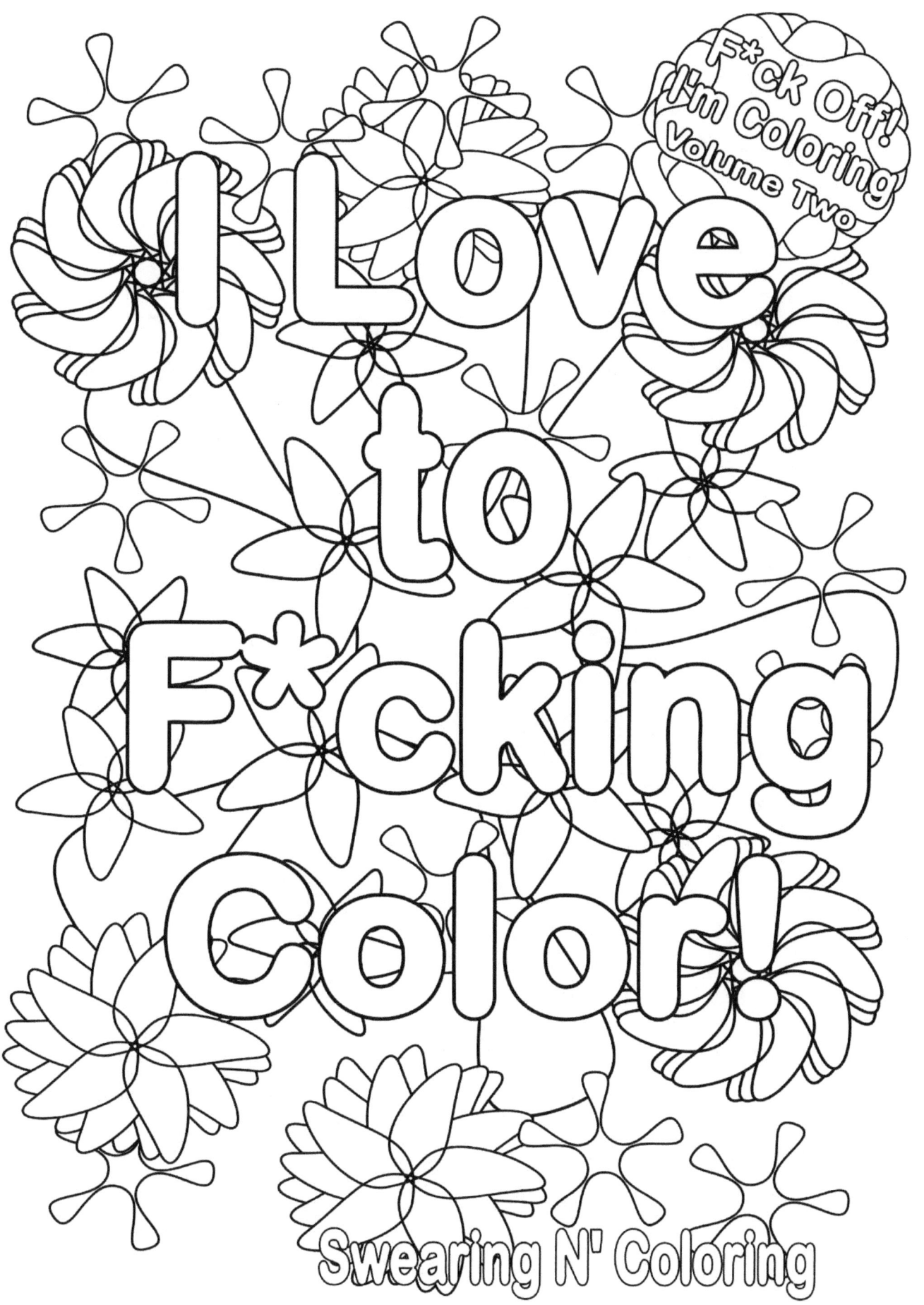